RACE WITH THE DEVIL

RACE WITH THE DEVIL

My Journey from Racial Hatred to Rational Love

JOSEPH PEARCE

SAINT BENEDICT PRESS
Charlotte, North Carolina

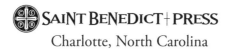

Joseph Pearce

Cataloging-in-Publication data on file with the Library of Congress.

ISBN: 978-1-61890-065-4

Published in the United States by
Saint Benedict Press, LLC
PO Box 410487
Charlotte, NC 28241
www.saintbenedictpress.com

Printed and bound in the United States of America.

For Albert Arthur Pearce,
who accompanied me
on the Journey.

Requiescat in Pace.

CONTENTS

RACE WITH THE DEVIL

CHAPTER 1

A SOUL IN SOLITARY CONFINEMENT

IT WAS the darkest day of my life.

I sat in a cell in London's Wormwood Scrubs prison on the second day of a twelve month prison sentence.

It was not the first time that I'd been to prison. Four years earlier I had served a six month sentence. In both cases I was imprisoned for publishing material deemed likely to incite racial hatred, a "hate crime" under Britain's Race Relations Act. I was a leading member of the National Front, a white supremacist organization that demanded the forced removal of all non-whites from the United Kingdom. I was also the editor of *Bulldog*, the newspaper of the Young National Front, and it was for publishing this journal that I was sentenced to prison on both occasions. There was, however, a huge difference between the twenty-year-old fanatic who had gone to prison four years earlier and the twenty-four-year-old who now sat in utter desolation in a lonely cell, less than two weeks before Christmas in 1985.

Back in January 1982 I had screamed defiantly at the judge who had sentenced me, warning him as I was dragged from the courtroom by the prison guards that the day would come when he would face his own judgment at the hands of the British people. In those days I had been an idealistic fanatic, and I considered myself a political prisoner of an anti-British tyrannical state. I had seen the first prison sentence as an act of willing self-sacrifice for the cause of racial liberation. I began a rigorous regimen of physical exercise, using the bed of my cell as an impromptu gym, scrambling under it to bench press my way into physical shape. I saw myself as a political soldier and a political prisoner who needed to emerge from jail in better shape physically and mentally for the renewal of the struggle. Secretly, in the solitude of my cell, I wrote my first book, a slim volume entitled *Fight for Freedom*, which I smuggled out with me at the end of my sentence, hiding the handwritten pages within the envelopes of the letters that I'd received. I was at war with Britain's multi-racial society, working tirelessly to bring it to its knees through the incitement of a race war from which the National Front would emerge, phoenix-like, from the ashes. Such was the strategy which had animated my actions and which had led to my imprisonment.

Much had happened, however, in the intervening four years and it was a very different person who began the second sentence in December 1985. As I looked despondently at the unmentionable abyss of time that the following twelve months represented, it was as though I were descending into a tunnel from which the light at the end was not yet visible. I did not know it but I was entering the dark night of the soul of which St. John of the Cross speaks. Nor did I know that this very day, December 14, was St. John of the Cross's feast day and that he had written his famous poem about the soul's dark night whilst he was himself languishing in prison, though in his case for a much worthier cause. Neither did I know that St. John of the Cross had finished writing his famous treatise on the dark night of the soul in 1585, exactly four hundred years earlier. At the time, I had never heard of this great religious poet who, a few short years later, would be one of the most important guides as I made my final approach to reception into the Catholic Church.

The previous day, the first full day of my sentence, had been the feast of St. Lucy, patroness of the blind. It was a singularly appropriate date for one so blinded by bigotry to begin his dark night of imprisonment and his journey towards the light of liberation that it would signify. I was indeed a blind man, oblivious of the saints' days on which the miracle of conversion was being wrought, ignorant of the intercession of the saints of whose presence I was unaware, and unable to see the hand of Providence in these coincidences. I had no light in my inner darkness except for the desire for a light I could not see. In the paradoxical light of such darkness, no words suffice to encapsulate my situation at the time better than the words of St. John of the Cross himself:

> Upon that lucky night
> In secrecy, inscrutable to sight,

I went without discerning
And with no other light
Except for that which in my heart
was burning.*

It was thus that I found myself fingering the rosary beads that someone had given me during the previous week's trial. Throughout my life, such beads had been an object of contempt, a mark of the superstitious Mariolatry of the Papists. My father often referred to Catholics as "bead rattlers." One day, when I was a boy, he had returned home from the pub and thrown my grandmother's rosary beads out of the window, declaring that we would not have such "papist beads" in the house. My maternal grandmother, Margaret Kavanagh, had hailed from County Galway, and my mother had brought the rosary home as a memento following her own mother's death in 1969. My mother never would have used the rosary for its intended purpose. Indeed she would not have known how to say the rosary even if she had wanted to. She and her eight siblings had all been brought up as nominal Anglicans, never going to church except for weddings and funerals. It was said that my grandfather cast his wife's priest from their home, shortly after their marriage, after the priest had urged that their children be raised Catholic. I like to believe that my grandmother sometimes told her beads, and I've heard that she occasionally went to Mass. If true, she would have been alone when she did so. All of her children

* From St. John of the Cross, "Upon a Gloomy Night," translated by Roy Campbell.

were brought up, like most nominal Anglicans, as de facto agnostics.

The anti-Catholicism that I had learned at my father's knee was deepened and darkened by my involvement with the Protestant Loyalists of Northern Ireland. I had travelled to Ulster on many occasions over the previous few years, at the very height of the Troubles which would claim almost four thousand lives before the Good Friday peace agreement was signed in 1998. I had joined the Orange Order, an anti-Catholic secret society, and had fraternized with members of Loyalist terrorist organizations, such as the Ulster Defence Association (UDA) and the Ulster Volunteer Force (UVF). As an Orangeman I knew many anti-Catholic songs, including a sectarian song berating the use of the rosary and celebrating the date on which the Protestants defeated the Catholic King James II at the Battle of the Boyne in 1690. Rather incongruously, it was sung to the tune of "Home on the Range":

> No, no Pope of Rome,
> No chapels to sadden my eyes;
> No nuns and no priests,
> No rosary beads,
> Every day is the Twelfth of July.

Yes, I knew all about rosary beads—or thought that I did. Now, however, sitting in my prison cell, I had no desire to emulate my father's example by throwing the beads out of the window. Nothing, in fact, could be further from my thoughts or my wishes. What I desired, more than anything, was to pray the rosary, to enter into its mysteries.

The problem, however, was the seemingly impenetrable wall of ignorance that separated me from it. I did not know the mysteries of the rosary. I did not even know the basic prayers of the rosary. I did not know the Apostles' Creed, the Hail Mary, or the Glory Be, and although I had been taught the Lord's Prayer as a child I had long since forgotten it. It would seem, therefore, that the mysteries I sought were beyond my reach. And yet, undaunted, I began to fumble the beads and mumble inarticulate prayers. It was the first time I had ever prayed. The results were nothing short of astonishing. The eyes of faith began to open, albeit with a vision that was more misty than mystical, and a hand of healing began to caress my hardened heart into a softness which would make it more malleable. I went to Mass for the first time in Wormwood Scrubs prison, and continued to go occasionally on Sundays after my transfer to Standford Hill, the prison in Kent in which I would serve the remainder of my sentence.

I still had a long way to travel and it would take a further three years before I would finally be received into the Catholic Church. I was, however, taking real though faltering steps in the right direction.

Although I was a long way from conversion, I was even further from the militant and fanatical racist who had gone to prison four years earlier. The intervening period and the change of mind and heart which had occurred is perhaps the most important part of a journey which could be considered a race with the devil. Those crucial years might be seen as the purgatorial ascent from racial hatred to rational love, the part of the journey in which the silver lining of redemptive possibility can be seen at the edge of every storm-laden cloud. Before such a purgatorial ascent can be attempted, however, we need to follow the downward path from childhood innocence into the infernal bowels of a hate-filled youth, plumbing the depths of anger and plummeting into the abyss of bigotry.

CHAPTER 2

A CHILDHOOD IN THE SHIRE

I WAS standing at the foot of the stairs, whining to my father because he wouldn't let me go upstairs to see why my mother was so unhappy. I could hear loud screams from my parents' bedroom and could not understand what was happening. In an effort to distract my attention and keep me happy, my father kept giving me chocolates from the Christmas tree. Sometime later, after my mother's distressed yells had ceased, I was taken upstairs and saw my newborn baby brother for the first time. He was being given his first bath and for a long time afterwards I believed that he had been born in the bath itself. It was Boxing Day 1962, the day after Christmas, my earliest memory. I was twenty-two months old.

My parents had intended to name my brother John, but the Irish midwife reminded them that the day of his birth was St. Stephen's Day and persuaded them to name him Stephen instead.

Steve was born in Haverhill, a small town in Suffolk, sixty-five miles north of London, to which my parents had moved a few months earlier. Previously, since their marriage in October 1957, they had lived in Ilford, on the edge of London's East End. It was here, or, to be precise, in the neighboring borough of Barking, that I was born on February 12, 1961, the first of their two children.

Haverhill had been a quaint agricultural market town for centuries on end, largely unchanged and unchanging, until it was designated as a site for London "overspill," its population burgeoning as Londoners moved there by the thousand throughout the 1960s. We were in the first wave of these urban migrants to the countryside, which meant that Haverhill still had the feel of a village during the years of my childhood.

I remember the 1960s as a time of idyllic innocence, not dissimilar in its rustic simplicity to the idealized England visualized by J. R. R. Tolkien in his depiction of the Shire. It would not, in fact, be the least exaggeration to say that my early formative years were spent in Arcadia. Plucking halcyon memories at random, I recall harvested fields as playgrounds, woods as places of adventure, trees as challenges to be climbed, and ponds as places to cool off on hot summer days. In those days hay bales were hobbit-sized, enabling us to build labyrinthine houses from these straw-blocks, through which we crawled, over which we climbed, and from which we jumped. Within walking distance were Ladywood and Bluebell wood, both of which became Sherwood Forest as we rode imaginary horses to escape the Sheriff of Nottingham and his evil cohorts. Another favorite destination was the newt pond, from which newts were caught with ease and in abundance. These we brought home in buckets and kept as pets, which my mother didn't mind, though she was less happy when I arrived home one day with a dead grass-snake.

We explored the surrounding countryside, taking long walks to exciting locations, such as an overgrown machine-gun post, a relic of the Second World War, into the dankness and darkness of which we descended in spite of the fear of the rats and other scary creatures which we felt must live there. Further along the same country road, devoid in those days of traffic, was a row of derelict houses, full of the detritus of the human families that had once breathed life into the now neglected and crumbling bricks and mortar. There was a tingling thrill attached to gatecrashing these domains of ghostly families long since departed. We told ourselves, or perhaps we were told by adults, that the ruined houses had been bombed during the War, a catastrophic possibility that added extra supernatural spice in the form of spectral victims of a violent and unexpected death. Were they sleeping in their beds when doomsday struck? Looking back, in the cold and distant light of day, I wonder why on earth the Luftwaffe would drop bombs on these isolated houses. And yet stray bombs did fall in the most unlikely places, and sometimes they were simply jettisoned as planes returned from missions with their deadly load still on board and without having reached their intended target. Did a bomb intended for London, Coventry, or some other city fall out of the darkness onto the houses of these unsuspecting country bumpkins, or was there a more prosaic explanation for the row of houses falling into ruin? I did not know then and am none the wiser now.

Another mysterious destination, about seven miles from Haverhill and within reach on our bikes, was Bartlow, the site of three ancient Roman burial mounds dating from the first or second century, during the early days of the Roman occupation of Britain. Such historical facts, if known to us, were embellished in our imaginations so that we believed that they were in fact the burial sites of three mysterious kings, enlarged in our mind's eye to Arthurian grandeur. Needless to say, we believed that the mounds were haunted, which gave an additional thrill as we dared each other to approach the dreaded spot.

Summer and autumn was scrumping season, during which we descended like a band of brigands or pirates on the neighboring orchards, pillaging plums, pears, apples, and strawberries as each fruit ripened, or often before they ripened. The ensuing stomach aches were attributed by my mother to the gluttonous quantity of fruit that we had consumed or the fact that it was not yet ripe, but I fancy that it may also have been due to the ingestion of the noxious chemicals that farmers by the 1960s were beginning to spray on their crops. Needless to say, we ate as we plucked and never thought about washing the fruit before consuming it.

It is odd that we gained such pleasure from this theft of the farmers' crops. There was a thrill to be had in climbing the fence into the orchard, in trespassing on someone else's property, in the risk of being caught, in the plucking of the forbidden fruit, in the eating of it. I am reminded in adulthood of St. Augustine's conscience-driven memory, recounted in his *Confessions*, of his own scrumping expedition as a child. He recalls "a pear tree laden with fruit" near his childhood home and the night-time raids that he and his friends made upon it. "We took enormous quantities, not to feast on ourselves but perhaps to throw to the pigs; we did eat a few, but that was not our motive: we derived pleasure from the deed simply because it was forbidden."*

St. Augustine's timely and timeless musings on the presence of concupiscence in the heart of youth serves to remind us that the innocence of childhood is not synonymous with the absence of sin. The Arcadia in which we resided was not Eden. Although we lived in blissful ignorance of the nature and magnitude of the adult sins that surrounded us, we could indulge in our own childish forms of it and did so with devilish delight. As sons of Adam we were willing apprentices in the antediluvian art of sin and became more adept in our practice of it as we got older but no wiser. It is for this reason that fairytales play such a healthy part in childhood. It is necessary for children to know that fairyland contains dragons, giants, and wicked witches because the real world contains grown-up versions of these evil creatures of which children need to have at least an inkling.

I remember my parents repeatedly telling me and my brother that we should not accept sweets from strangers and that we should not get into a stranger's car. When we asked why we should not do so, we were simply told that

---

* Saint Augustine of Hippo, *The Confessions*, San Francisco: Ignatius Press, 2012, p. 41

there were "funny men" and that we had to beware of them. No doubt my parents' concern was accentuated and exacerbated by the horrific case of the Moors Murderers, Ian Brady and Myra Hindley, who had sexually assaulted and murdered five children in horrific circumstances between 1963 and 1965. Their trial in 1966, when I was five-years-old, shocked the world with the sickeningly sadistic nature of the killings, the details of which must have struck terror into the hearts of every parent of young children.

The case of the Moors Murderers, of which I knew nothing at the time, illustrates the abyss which separated the carefree and wide-eyed world of childhood in which I lived with the wickedness of the wider world beyond. The sixties were a time of tumult and turmoil of which my friends and I were mercifully unaware. Little did we know it—or could we know it—but our little Arcadia was a place of peace and stillness in the midst of a maelstrom. I was living in the eye of the storm.

CHAPTER 3

THE GHOSTS OF THE PAST

FLANNERY O'CONNOR wrote of the American South that it was "hardly Christ-centered" but that it was "certainly Christ haunted."* It would be equally true to describe England as Christ-haunted, though in England's case it would be truer to say that the ghost of Christ is considered an unwelcome guest, a shade or shadow of the past who refuses to go away. Thus it was that the faded figure of Christ overshadowed my own childhood, although, as with so much else, I did not know it at the time. The shadow of His presence and the presence of His Church was everywhere, though in a form that had been grotesquely distorted by the defamation and deformation that was the consequence of England's break from Rome. It might, in fact, be truer to say that Christ's faded presence was itself overshadowed by the fading presence of the English Reformation and the anti-papist propaganda that it spawned.

---

* Flannery O'Connor, *Mystery and Manners: Occasional Prose*, New York: Farrar, Straus and Giroux, 1969, p. 44

This, at least, is the impression that emerges as I survey the cultural landscape of my childhood, eyeing it with the wisdom of hindsight across the abyss of years that separate me from it.

Take, for instance, the name of one of the woods in which my friends and I used to play. We believed that Ladywood was so named because it had once belonged to a grand, mediaeval Lady. Our fecund imagination conceived a tragic tale involving her untimely death, which, in consequence, meant that the wood was haunted by the restless spirit of her unhappy ghost. The prospect of encountering the Lady's spectral presence in the darkness of the woods added a chilling thrill to our adventures. The presence of such a ghostly legend cast a shadow over the likely truth that "Ladywood" was probably the colloquial abbreviation of "Our Lady's Wood," the name with which our Catholic ancestors had baptized it, dedicating it to the Mother of God. Thus the shadow of Mary had been overshadowed by later legends that had eclipsed her mystical presence. As I think of how Mary had been exiled from the very place that had been dedicated to her, of how she had been culturally evicted from English history, and how she had been denied her place in my childhood imagination, I am reminded of Mary's words in John Henry Newman's lament for the plight of "The Pilgrim Queen":

> "And me they bid wander
> in weeds and alone,
> In this green merry land
> Which once was my own."

Unconsciously my friends and I had inherited a subliminal anti-Catholicism, which manifested itself in an irrational fear of monks. On one occasion we dared each other to break into what we believed was a deserted monastery on the edge of town. The only access was through a broken hatch leading into the cellar. We descended cagily into the gloom and found our way up the stairs into the main building. It was empty except for a few old hymn books. In retrospect, as my mind's eye surveys the scene, it is evident that the building could not have been empty for long. I also have my doubts about whether it was ever a monastery, though it clearly had some religious use. In any event, we filled the vacuum created by our ignorance with a vision of "ghostly friars" very different from the Shakespearean meaning of the term. Clearly the building must be haunted and equally clearly the ghostly friars would not be holy spirits. Spooking each other into a state of hysteria we beat a hasty retreat through the gloom of the cellar, which seemed much scarier on the way out than it had on the way in!

Our morbid fascination with the dead, or the undead, found further expression in the playing of the Ouija board at the instigation of a boy four years our senior, whom I suspected then, and am convinced now, orchestrated proceedings by moving the glass which we used as an improvised planchette. This boy, no doubt having great fun at our expense, told us that the greatest thing to fear was making contact with the three worst spirits imaginable, namely Satan, Hitler, and the Mad Monk. The first of this decidedly unholy trinity is understandable enough, as is the addition of Hitler, but it is a little odd that the third most evil entity imaginable should be the spirit of a monk, albeit a "mad" one. We knew that the Mad Monk's name was Rasputin and that he was Russian, but our scanty knowledge had its roots in Hollywood and not in history.

A further manifestation of the implicit anti-Catholicism of the culture of our youth was the annual celebration of Guy Fawkes Night, or bonfire night, instigated as a rather perverse "holy day" by the Anglican Church and the English Parliament in the wake of the so-called Gunpowder Plot of 1605. Thereafter, Guy Fawkes night was celebrated annually on November 5, the anniversary of the discovery of the plot. It involved fireworks and the building of bonfires, upon the latter of which an effigy of Guy Fawkes, one of the perpetrators of the plot, was burned. Every year, as Guy Fawkes Night approached, we would stuff old clothes with rags or newspaper, and place one of the mass-produced Guy Fawkes masks on a papier maché orb, which served as the effigy's head. We would then sit outside shops begging the passers-by for "a penny for the Guy." On the night itself, our "Guy" would be placed on top of the family's bonfire and we would watch it burn as fireworks were set off in celebration. In other parts of the country it is also customary to burn effigies of the pope and other *bêtes noires*. At Lewes in Sussex a huge effigy of the current pope is burned every year along with one other present-day hate figure. Sometime in the 1980s, at the height of my own anti-Catholicism, I made a "pilgrimage" to Lewes on Guy Fawkes Night and was delighted to see giant effigies of John Paul II and Ronald Reagan paraded past the gathering crowd of on-lookers en route to the two bonfires on which they were ceremoniously burned to the accompaniment of drunken jeers and cheers.

The remnant of a healthier past was celebrated each year in the lingering traditions of Christendom.

My parents had a healthily rambunctious and Dickensian love for Christmas. This meant that our family Christmases were interwoven with sacrosanct traditions and rituals, including the annual excitement of putting up the decorations, hanging up the Christmas cards, and decorating the tree. It was as though the Ghost of Christmas Past revisited every year, along with Santa Claus, to ensure the continuation of family tradition. My brother and I were always lavished with a mountain of gifts, which we opened in an orgy of ecstatic abandon as our parents looked on with delight. The annual debauch was not that dissimilar to the scene in *A Christmas Story* in which Ralphie and Randy open their presents as their parents observe the proceedings with rekindled, childlike eyes. This wonderful film is not well-known in England and I had never seen it before I moved to America. Yet its depiction of the family on Christmas Day brought back the happiest of memories. The age difference between Ralphie and Randy is about the same as that between me and my brother and the evident disdain with which the brothers discover that one of their wrapped presents contained only new socks resonates with the way that I felt upon the discovery of socks, underpants, and handkerchiefs. These anti-climactic gifts were quickly discarded in the quest for more interesting and exciting treasures.

Another, less edifying parallel with *A Christmas Story* was the relative absence of Christ from our Christmases. There was never any mention of going to church. It was not something that either of my parents had ever been in the practice of doing and this tradition of religious indifference, no doubt inherited from their parents, was handed down to their own children in turn. Nor was their indifference the least unusual. Of all of my friends, and I had many, I was only aware of one of them going to church, and he was the son of Irish Catholic parents who took him each Sunday to the small, newly-built Catholic church, which could be seen from our front door. As for the rest of us, nominally Anglican, or "C of E" as we labeled ourselves when asked, we never darkened the door of a church unless someone was getting married.

Religious indifference, with its inherent tendency towards agnosticism, is, however, not synonymous with an antagonism towards religion. Whereas atheists are antagonistic towards religion because they are anything but indifferent towards it, my parents saw Christianity as being good and benign, even if it shouldn't be taken too seriously. As for atheism, I'm sure that my parents would have seen it as mean-spirited, the creed of killjoy Scrooges who refused the brotherhood of man implicit in the spirit of Christmas.

My mother loved the traditional Christmas carols, and my father, when inebriated after Christmas festivities at the local pub, would serenade us with a slurred rendition of "Silent Night" in its original German. On such occasions he would also remind us solemnly that we were Christians, though this seemed primarily a tribal badge, distinguishing us from Jews or Muslims. To be fair, he occasionally cited passages from Scripture, especially the Gospels, and he would (as would my mother), if pressed, have confessed Christ as his Saviour and Lord. It was simply that this tacit acceptance of residual Christianity did not imply any active participation through prayer or other signs of religious observance.

Other examples of residual Christianity and the lingering shadow of Christendom included my mother's annual baking of pancakes on Pancake Day, which we looked forward to each year. Pancake Day took place on Shrove Tuesday, or Mardi Gras, but was otherwise unconnected with its wider meaning as the final day before the solemn onset of the Lenten season of penance. Similarly, my mother made hot cross buns on Good Friday as a surviving remnant of the ritualistic expression of the significance of the day of Christ's Crucifixion. On Easter Sunday we would be given chocolate eggs but there was never any question of celebrating Christ's Resurrection by attending church, or even by so much as a solitary prayer of thanksgiving. Looking back, it all seems somewhat odd. At the time, however, this was the norm by which all else was judged.

In those days, secular fundamentalism had not yet tightened its vice-like grip on public life and Place Farm Primary School, which I attended from the ages of four to eleven, still paid lip service to Christianity. At school assembly we parotted the Lord's Prayer as a compulsory part of the school day but I have no recollection of religion playing any other part in my formal education. Occasionally, on Sundays, the Salvation Army band would appear on the street corner, a cause of some excitement to the children of the neighborhood. As the band marched off in uniform, playing their instruments as they went, we followed on like those who followed the Pied Piper.

Although the local Catholic church was on the other side of the street from our house, its presence was almost imperceptible. We paid little attention to those who arrived for Mass each Sunday, though I recall my father being amused when one of his friends referred to the Mass-goers as "sanctimonious bastards." The only time that the life of the church entered our own lives was during its annual fête, held in the surrounding field. We descended upon this hub of activity like bees round honey, wandering from stall to stall and sampling the food on offer. A highlight for me was the game that the father of my solitary Catholic friend set up each year. It involved a drainpipe, positioned vertically, down which an imitation rat would be dropped. The idea was to hit the rat with a stick before it hit the ground. It was great fun, and much more difficult than it seemed.

There was, however, one religious experience at this church, which affected me profoundly at the time and which came back to haunt me as I recalled it to memory many years later. One of my friends, a girl of my age, expressed a serious interest in becoming a Catholic. We were only nine or ten at the time and it seems odd, in retrospect, that a girl of such an age should feel prompted toward religious conversion. It was even odder because it was her father who had scorned the local Catholics for being sanctimonious and her brother who had tempted us to dabble in diabolism with the Ouija board. In any event, at her beckoning

I went with her into the neighboring church, something I had never done previously in spite of my natural curiosity and in spite of its proximity to my house. She showed me around, pointing to the various statues with the utmost reverence and seriousness. My only clear recollection of this singular episode was the deep impression it left of the real presence of God. I had been in Protestant churches, including the fourteenth-century Anglican church of St. Mary in the center of town, and had experienced no such sense of God's presence. This might have had something to do with the barrenness of St. Mary's interior, which had been stripped by the Puritans of all of its religious art and images during the Civil War, but I wonder now whether it might have been connected to the Real Presence of Christ in the tabernacle. I knew nothing of such things at the time so such a Presence could only have been perceived through the infusion of grace. Or perhaps I was simply moved aesthetically by the beauty and piety of the statues and other art adorning the walls, windows, and sanctuary. Whatever the reason, the small and modern Catholic church, so ugly and unimpressive on the outside, had something within it which the majestic and venerable St. Mary's, so beautiful on the outside, utterly lacked. I was to experience something similar a couple of years later when one of my cousins was married in a Catholic church. Psychologically, if these things can be explained in such terms, it was strange that I felt this peculiar "real presence" during my two brief visits to Catholic churches whereas there was nothing but a real absence in any of the old Anglican churches that I entered, and this in spite of my love of history which should have predisposed me to prefer the older edifices over the new.

My friend never asked me to accompany her to the church again and, as far as I know, her attraction to Catholicism was merely a passing fad. For my part, I soon forgot the whole episode, allowing it to settle somewhere in the remotest recesses of my mind from which it would emerge as a revitalized revelation many years later, a ghost from the past as surprising and astonishing in its resurrection in the mind of the man as it had been in its original incarnation in the heart of the boy.

CHAPTER 4

IN MY FATHER'S IMAGE

DURING THIS whole period of my childhood the greatest influence upon me was my father. For the most part, in spite of some of the less flattering depictions of him already presented, I have nothing but gratitude to him for all the good things he taught me and all the love that he bestowed upon me. Although it was said by Wordsworth that the child is father of the man, it would be fair to say in my case that the child who is father of the man is the man he is because of the father of the child. To put the matter less convolutedly, I am largely who I am because of who my father was. I was made in his image. I would add, however, that my own journey would be largely defined and delineated by my rejection of many of my father's beliefs. This being so, it would be remiss of me to conclude the account of my childhood without paying due attention to my father's influence.

Born in 1930 in a London borough adjacent to the one in which I would be born thirty-one years later, my father, Albert Arthur Pearce, had his own childhood rudely interrupted by the eruption of the Second World War.

He was evacuated, first to Norfolk and then to Somerset, to escape the dangers and horrors of the Nazi blitzkrieg. Having spent part of his childhood away from his family in enforced exile in the English countryside, he left school at fourteen, having never really excelled as a student, and became a carpenter, following in his own father's footsteps. Referring to his craft, he used to quip somewhat mischievously that there was only ever one good carpenter and that He had been crucified for His labors.

He grew up with all the pride and prejudice of a child of the British Empire, devoted to the pomp and circumstance of British imperial tradition, and was embittered by witnessing its dissolution and decay during his own lifetime. His own father had been born during the reign of Queen Victoria, when the Empire was at its zenith and when it was said quite correctly that the sun never set upon it. The emasculation of Britain in the twentieth century was a bitter pill for my father to swallow. He held on to the romantic vision of the Empire long after it had ceased to exist in reality. He proclaimed with bombastic bravura that there were only three types of people in the world: Englishmen, those who would like to be Englishmen, and those who didn't know any better. I always felt a little uncomfortable at the arrogance of such a statement but I embraced the belief that the British or the English (the words were always used interchangeably and synonymously) were somehow a chosen people, a people set apart. We were somehow better than everyone else.

Like the rest of his generation, and like many preceding generations, he had been brought up on what Hilaire

Belloc described disparagingly as "tom-fool Protestant history," the "enormous mountain of ignorant wickedness" which the Whig historians had erected to justify the English Reformation and its aftermath.* This accounted, in part, for my father's negative view of Catholicism and his berating of Catholics as "bead-rattlers." Such inherent anti-Catholicism was exacerbated by his youthful confrontation with Irish immigrants in London. As a young man, he was involved in many a pub brawl with Irishmen, provoked no doubt by the festering political enmity that existed between the two warring peoples, and he sported a scar on his lip from one such encounter with a burly Dubliner. This volcano of vindictiveness against the Irish erupted with new and vitriolic force with the onset of the Troubles in Northern Ireland in the late-sixties.

Coupled with my father's hostility to the Irish was his resentment of the negative consequences of mass immigration to England in the aftermath of the 1948 British Nationality Act. This was quite literally changing the complexion of the country. In my father's view, the effects of multi-racialism were disastrous, threatening the very future of British nationhood and British national identity. This was a view that I would come to embrace also, though not until a few years later when I began to think in terms of politics.

This depiction of my father's pride and prejudice presents an image of the man which is not only unflattering

---

* Hilaire Belloc to Hoffman Nickerson, 13 September 1923; Belloc Collection, Boston College: Quoted in Joseph Pearce, *Old Thunder: A Life of Hilaire Belloc*, San Francisco: Ignatius Press, 2002, p. 230

but also only partially true. Although these were indeed his views, it fails to show the extent that my father genuinely loved his fellow man. Although he vented his spleen against the Irish, many of his closest friends were Irishmen. He drank with them in the pubs that he frequented. He worked with them. He joked with them. My father was not like the philanthropist who proclaims his love for Man but despises men. Indeed he was the opposite of the philanthropist. He loved men but despised those who spoke in the abstract about the brotherhood of man. A communist, my father said, is one who demands that you be his brother or else he'll crack your skull. Having nothing but contempt for such abstract notions of "brotherhood," my father was a brother to everyone he met and rejoiced in the conviviality and conversation to be found in their company. He railed against the Irishman in the abstract but embraced the Irishman in the pub, his youthful brawls notwithstanding. In spite of all appearances to the contrary, few men loved their fellow men more fully and more truly and with such Dickensian and Chestertonian exuberance as did my father. This may seem paradoxical perhaps but it is a paradox that must be embraced and understood if we are to understand the man who molded my early life more than any other.

Another aspect of my father's life and personality that I have sought to emulate is his omnivorous love of knowledge. Having left school at such a young age, and having failed to excel in the little formal education that he had, he followed the path of the autodidact to an extraordinary degree. He knew the capital city and the flag of every country in the world and was irritated when nations changed them. He knew the name of every county town in England and the name of every state capital in the United States. He had taught himself the military history of England and waxed lyrical about English victories against the French at Agincourt or against the Scots at Culloden. He could recite the whole of the speeches before the battles of Harfleur and Agincourt from Shakespeare's *Henry V* and knew Tennyson's "Charge of the Light Brigade" in its entirety. My father revered Shakespeare, a reverence that I have inherited, and could also quote the whole of Portia's "quality of mercy" speech from *The Merchant of Venice*. Although Portia's speech is about mercy, the necessity of forgiveness, and the dangers of the theology of vengeance implicit in the demand for "an eye for an eye" or "a pound of flesh," there is also a suggestion of anti-Semitism in her words which my father found attractive.*

My father was anti-Semitic in much the same way that he was anti-Irish and I have no doubt that he would have loved the Jewish people whom he met as he loved the Irishmen with whom he worked and drank. He believed that there was a Jewish problem as he believed that there was an Irish problem or an immigrant problem, but he would never have countenanced a "final solution" along the lines of that attempted by the Nazis. He loved people too much to sanction their extermination. Nonetheless, he had what I

* At least, such a suggestion is often suggested by critics. For the dangers and errors of ascribing a conventional understanding of anti-Semitism to Shakespeare, see my discussion of the issue in *Through Shakespeare's Eyes* (Ignatius Press, 2010).

now consider to be an unhealthy admiration for Germany, which, as a youth, I would come to share. Although he was proud of the success of the British army during the Second World War and would often quote Churchill's famous speeches, which he also seemed to have learned by heart, he came to have a creeping sympathy for Hitler and would also quote Churchill's alleged quip after the Iron Curtain had fallen across Europe that the allies had slain the wrong pig, i.e., that Stalin's communism was even worse than Hitler's National Socialism.

My father's loathing of communism was so intense that it was easy to slip into the quagmire of believing that my enemy's enemy is my friend. Hitler's anti-communism trumped the less savory aspects of his politics, leading my father to romanticize about the heroism of the SS on the Eastern Front, fighting against the hated Reds. This romantic revisionism was accentuated by his friendship with an Estonian, whom he had met in a local pub and who had fought with the SS during the war. Having taught himself German, my father also learned all the words to the *Horst Wessel Lied*, the official Nazi Party anthem, which he would sometimes sing after returning from the pub. My father's singing of this notorious song, banned in Germany since the War, sits uncomfortably beside *Stille Nacht* (Silent Night), the other song that he was in the habit of singing in German, especially when drunk. The incongruity of the spirit of these two songs is emblematic of the contradictions at the heart of my father's *weltanschauung.* He was, at one and the same time, a sort of Christian who was not fully Christian and a sort of Nazi who was not really a Nazi.

My father could sing a Christmas carol without feeling the desire to go to church at Christmas and he could sing a Nazi Party anthem without the desire to attend a political rally or support any particular political party.

Many years later, when I found myself in a crowded cellar bar in the German city of Kleve, surrounded by a hostile group of young Germans, I was grateful for having learned the *Horst Wessel Lied* from my father. There was a British army base close to Kleve and, unbeknownst to me, there was a culture of hostility between the British soldiers and the German youth of the city, no doubt fuelled by a history of bar brawls between the rival groups. The fact that I was evidently English, and had a brawny appearance and a close-shaved head, led the aggressive group of drunken Germans to the not unreasonable conclusion that I must be a soldier. I was surrounded by hostile heads screaming at me in a language that I did not understand. Unable to communicate in any other way and sensing the neo-fascist orientation of the mob, I burst into a rendition of the *Horst Wessel Lied*, simultaneously raising my arm in a Nazi salute. The effect was astonishing. The group fell into a confused silence as they stared in disbelief as *der Engländer* sang the illegal anthem of the Third Reich. Those who could speak English asked me how I knew the song and an air of friendship prevailed thereafter. Instead of finding myself attacked and perhaps beaten senseless, I found myself being patted on the back and bought beers. Perversely my knowledge of that which was *verboten* had saved the day!

It seems inescapable in the light of the journey that I am recounting that I should dwell on those aspects of my father's character and those facets of his beliefs that would have such a potent impact on my own descent into political extremism. Yet such a focus does not do him justice. If I can attribute some of my errors to my father's influence, I can attribute most of my redeeming qualities to his influence also. He lavished his love upon me and I cannot lay at his door the least accusation of abuse. On the contrary, the extent to which I love my fellow man is attributable, under grace, to the example my father gave me. My love of poetry and history also has its roots in his love for these things. My omnivorous hunger for knowledge is a gift that he gave me. The path of the autodidact, which he took through life, is the path that I have followed also. I am happy to have followed in my father's footsteps, though equally happy that I ceased to do so when I came to realize that he was not always walking in the right direction.

As I conclude this candid exposition of the extent to which I was made in my father's image, I'd like to accentuate the positive, which it is all too easy to forget. The most evocative way in which I can do so is to recall another of my father's favorite poems, Thomas Gray's "Elegy written in a Country Churchyard," which he had learned by heart and which he would recite in moments of melancholy and sober reflection. For those who know this wonderful poem, the very fact that my father admired it and had consigned it to loving memory will be enough to exonerate him. The epitaph with which Gray ends the poem will serve as my own final words on the goodness of my father's heart:

Here rests his head upon the lap of Earth
A Youth to Fortune and to Fame unknown.
Fair Science frown'd not on his humble birth,
And Melancholy mark'd him for her own.

Large was his bounty, and his soul sincere,
Heav'n did a recompense as largely send:
He gave to Mis'ry all he had, a tear,
He gain'd from Heav'n ('twas all he wish'd)
a friend.

No farther seek his merits to disclose,
Or draw his frailties from their dread abode,
(There they alike in trembling hope repose,)
The bosom of his Father and his God.

CHAPTER 5

TO THINE OWN SELF BE TRUE

ALTHOUGH MUCH has been said of my father's potent presence in my life, the part that my mother played is much more difficult to discern or define. My parents were as different as chalk and cheese. My father was a thinker and astonishingly well-read whereas my mother contented herself with trashy romantic fiction and was unable to write a grammatical sentence. Whereas my father enjoyed the engagement of the intellect, and was a keen chess player, teaching me and my brother to play also, my mother was uninterested in any form of cerebral pursuit and could be described as a bundle of feelings, a teddy bear who gave love unthinkingly.

Above all else, my mother's life was centered on her family, on me and my brother as her immediate family but also on her extended family, most of whom were still in the area of East London where she had grown up. The eighth of nine children, she had a close relationship with her siblings and felt isolated in Haverhill, from which we were only able to travel to London about once a year. My parents never owned a car, indeed neither of them ever learned to drive, so the distance of sixty-five miles between our home in the countryside and the homes of my grandparents, aunts, uncles, and cousins, proved to be a major obstacle. Our annual bus trips to London were major highlights in our lives, as were the rare visits to Haverhill by those of our relatives who had cars.

My father had always insisted that we were Londoners, natives of the largest and proudest city in the world (which was no longer the case when he told us so), and he was constantly reminding me and my brother that we were not "carrot crunchers," the disparaging term he used for our country bumpkin neighbors. I remember his efforts to correct our accents when he detected hints of a rustic dialect creeping into our speech. I was, therefore, conscious of my cultural identity as a cockney even though I had lived in a small Suffolk country town all my life, or at least all of it that I was able to remember. It was for this reason that, at the age of around seven, I chose Chelsea as the soccer team to which I owed my allegiance, a passion that has remained with me to the present day. I knew that I had to pick a London side to support and that the local Suffolk team, Ipswich Town, was not an option, but I can't recall why I selected Chelsea instead of other top London clubs, such as Arsenal, Tottenham, or West Ham.

Harboring a sense of exile for a city in which I'd not lived since my infancy, I spied a notice in a local shop advertising a "house exchange" in which a family in Barking, the neighborhood in which I'd been born, sought to exchange homes with a family in Haverhill.* Excitedly I relayed the news to my parents. My mother leapt at the prospect of returning home to her own extended family but I was shocked to detect an air of hesitation, even panic, in my father. For all his talk of London and apparent disdain for "carrot crunchers," he had laid real roots in Haverhill and was reluctant to leave. Years later, I rather think that he looked back on the eleven years that we spent in Suffolk as the happiest of his life. There was, however, no dissuading my mother. Sensing the prospect of a return to her own family, she contacted the family in Barking and plans were made to exchange homes.

In August 1973, when I was twelve years old, we packed all of our belongings into a moving van and set off for our new home in the big city. My parents sat in the front with the driver, my brother and I sat in the back. As we pulled away and I watched all the familiar places receding into the distance, I think I was aware, even then, that I was watching my childhood disappear. Something was being left behind that could never be regained. Haverhill, the haven of my days of innocence, was passing away as surely as the days that I had lived there. The town had more than tripled in size in the decade since we'd first arrived and the expansion would continue. The newt pond is no more, having been filled in to make way for a housing development, and the numerous orchards have all been obliterated

* My parents never owned their own home and always lived in council housing, homes owned by local government authorities and rented to residents. It was possible to exchange homes with residents of council houses in other parts of the country.

by the European Union's dastardly and disastrous agricultural policy. The gardens from which I had plucked the forbidden fruit have disappeared as surely as the Garden in which our first parents had committed the original plucking. Exiled from the paradise of childhood, I was setting forth into a newer and darker world.

The first major impact of the move to our new home was that I now had to share a bedroom with Steve, my brother. Our home in Haverhill had three bedrooms, which had enabled me to have my own room. The new home had two bedrooms only. In retrospect, it seems odd that my parents would have agreed to exchange a three-bedroom home for a two bedroom replacement but I suspect the sacrifice of space was the price my mother was willing to make to have her own extended family as neighbors. The adjustment involved in getting used to sharing a room with my brother was as nothing compared with the adjustment involved in the experience of school. The schools in Haverhill had been small and friendly. There were relatively few disciplinary issues and an atmosphere of decorum prevailed. I had excelled in such an environment, being top or near-top of my class in most subjects. It might be something of an exaggeration were I to describe myself as a model student during my years at Place Farm primary school and Chalkstone middle school, but it would be true to say that I was well-adjusted and popular with both my peers and my teachers. All this was destined to change in the progressive atmosphere of Eastbury comprehensive school.

I recall my first day at the new school with a chilling vividness. The sheer size of the school and the teeming mass of returning students was something on a scale I had never experienced. I also felt very young. Every student seemed bigger and more grown-up than I was. I was a pygmy amongst giants; a child in the midst of adults. This was a new experience because I had been a very confident student in Haverhill and had the reputation of being one of the best fighters in the school (not that fights were common). Now I felt small and very vulnerable.

I was to be a first year, which at least meant that everyone else in my year was as new to the school as I was. It was clear, however, that most of them had already gravitated to friends from their own neighborhoods or from their previous schools. They might have been new to this particular environment but they were not alone. Rather timidly and cagily I attached myself to a group of boys who mercifully seemed willing to welcome me into their number. In a wrestling match with one of the boys in the school playing field I was surprised to discover that I was in fact stronger than he was. This helped to alleviate my sense of inferiority but did little to alter the impression that he and his friends were simply more mature, more grown-up. Imagine my shock, therefore, when I was called into the administrative office at lunchtime on my first day to be told that a mistake had been made and that I should have been enrolled with the second year class. Already feeling at least a year younger than the first years, I now found myself catapulted into the presence of students a year older still. It was as though I had been forced to become two years older in the space of a single morning. It also meant that I was genuinely the new kid on the block because all the other students in my class were returning for their second year and already sat in their customary cliques. The fact that I was introduced to the class in the middle of the day merely accentuated my sense of alienation.

Recounting this scene in the cold light of day, forty years after it happened, does nothing to bring home the psychological shock of the experience of being hurtled from childhood to adolescence almost overnight. It would be going too far to describe the day's events as traumatic but they did shake me up considerably. Indeed, those of a more timid or introverted disposition might have been turned into neurotic wrecks by the seismic shift in self-identity that this new urban and streetwise culture demanded. For my part, intent on survival, I shed the remnants of rustic innocence and adopted the cockiness of the cockney.

My descent into delinquency was aided and abetted by the progressive philosophy adopted by the school. No effort was made to impose discipline, which resulted in the triumph of anarchy in the classroom and the survival of the fittest in the playground. In the former, the disruptive elements made it difficult, if not impossible, for teachers to teach and for students to learn. In the latter, the school bully and his coterie of friends ruled the roost, making life miserable for everyone else and making playtime a time of fear.

I joined the disruptive elements and remember with lasting repugnance the war of attrition that I conducted against a young Pakistani mathematics teacher. My racism was now ripening into hatred and my English pride resented being subject to a non-white immigrant. I made this poor teacher's life hell, on one occasion throwing a chair at him and on another driving him to such fury that he lashed out and kicked me as he ejected me from the classroom. I remember the young man's name to this day, though I'm guessing he has to be in his mid-sixties now, and wish that I could apologize for my abominable behavior towards him.

In the playground I had no desire to become a bully myself, or to become one of the bully's cronies. I had gained from my father a sense of the honor and chivalry that should always be attached to the art of fighting. My father was something of a pugilist. He was not a big man but what he lacked in size and weight he gained in the rapidity with which he threw a jab. He taught me to box from the earliest age, though in a somewhat haphazard and occasional fashion, and spoke earnestly of how the Marquess of Queensberry Rules should be followed at all times, not only in the ring but wherever and whenever I found myself in a fight. There was to be no kicking or biting or pulling of hair, no hitting a man while he's down, and absolutely no use of knives and other weapons. To one degree or another I carried this gentlemanly philosophy with me during my street brawling years though I soon discovered how impractical it was in the presence of a violent mob.

Part of my father's pugilistic philosophy came from his contempt for the bully who preys upon the weak. With my father's martial light to guide me, I had no desire to join the bullies but nor was I prepared to become a victim. It became clear to the school bully pretty quickly, without the need for blows, that I was not easy pickings. He took the path of least resistance and left me alone. He was killed tragically whilst trespassing on a construction site a few months after my first encounter with him. I can't remember whether he fell to his death or was crushed under the weight of a heavy object. I do remember, however, how little he was mourned. It saddens me that someone could die so young and so unloved.

Although I suspect that the contempt with which I treated my teachers was due primarily to the general culture of anarchy that prevailed, it was accentuated by the animosity I felt towards the sort of education being offered. I had learned to loath communism at my father's knee and sensed the Marxist flavor of many of the lessons. My physics teacher openly confessed that he was a member of the International Marxist Group, though I'm not sure that it would have been very easy to insinuate a Marxist interpretation of the laws of thermodynamics! It was, however, much easier to insert a quasi-Marxist agenda into the teaching of history and literature.

A few years later, when I was about seventeen, I wrote an article for *Spearhead*, a magazine published by John Tyndall, the National Front's chairman and subsequently the founder of the British National Party, entitled "Red Indoctrination in the Classroom," which critiqued the Marxist orientation of my high school education. I noted that the only history that had been taught was British social history from 1815 to 1914. Being raised by my father on British military history, wherein I believed the glory of England was to be discovered, I was understandably perturbed by a teaching of my nation's history that concentrated solely on acts of Parliament and movements, mostly avowedly socialist, agitating for political reform. I even detected an implicit bias in the way in which the course began immediately after the glorious British victory at Waterloo, thereby avoiding discussion of other great British victories, such as that of the Royal Navy under the command of Lord Nelson, one of my father's great heroes, at Trafalgar in 1805. In similar vein, the ending of the course in 1914, just before the beginning of the First World War, avoided any mention of the sacrifices made for Britain and her Empire by the troops in the trenches.

My youthful and opinionated critique was justified, up to a point. The concentration on social history to the exclusion of everything else, especially in its exclusive focus on the cauldron of political and economic change in the nineteenth century, lent itself very conveniently to a Marxist reading of events, and I suspect that such was the intention of those who constructed the curriculum and designed the syllabus. On the other hand, of course, it never dawned on me that the education I had received from my father was equally biased in a jingoistic and imperialistic direction. My father had concentrated on English or British military victories to the exclusion of everything else. There was no mention of other major battles, such as the Siege of Troy, the Battle of Marathon, the fall of Roland at Roncesvalles, or the naval victory of Christendom at Lepanto. Regarding the last of these, I find it curious and significant that my father knew and loved Chesterton's poem "The Donkey," which he could recite from memory, but was apparently unaware of Chesterton's famous poem about Lepanto.

It was also significant that he spoke often of great victories, against the odds, such as Agincourt, or heroically tragic events such as the Charge of the Light Brigade, but that the defeat of the British in the American Revolution was passed over in embarrassed silence. I could detect the bias of my teachers, all of whom were presumed to be Marxists or fellow travelers, but I could not detect the bias of my own perspective. It was as though I was pointing out the mote in my brother's eye whilst ignoring the plank in mine.

My *Spearhead* article also condemned the way in which English literature was taught at my school. I complained about the perceived Marxist bias of the set texts, which included *Romeo and Juliet*, the war poetry of Wilfred Owen, *Animal Farm*, and *Chicken Soup with Barley*, the last of which, less well known, is a play by Arnold Wesker.

The selection of *Romeo and Juliet* was criticized because it implied a bias against the great history plays, such as *Henry V*. In my youthful judgment (and ignorance) the history plays highlighted the greatness of the English people, which the Marxists were at pains to studiously ignore. The selection of Wilfred Owen's war poetry was seen as an excuse to preach an anti-war message and to highlight the work of a coward who ridiculed the glory and honor of laying down one's life for one's country. Orwell's *Animal Farm* and Wesker's play were selected because they were nothing more than anti-fascist propaganda. Wasn't Orwell a communist who fought with the reds in the Spanish Civil War? Wasn't Wesker not only a communist but a Jew? What further proof was necessary that such work should not be allowed to sully the minds of impressionable youth? Such was the judgment of the angry teenager on the education that he had recently completed.

Although they were shrill, simplistic, and overstated, there was nonetheless a modicum of truth in my criticisms. *Romeo and Juliet*, along with *Julius Caesar*, is the most popular of Shakespeare's plays as a set text for high schools because it is one of the most accessible of the Bard's plays, much easier for a modern teenager to comprehend than *Henry V* or the other history plays. The setting of this text was, therefore, justified on solid pragmatic grounds. That being said, the play was taught from the perspective of the modern libertine romantic and was not therefore presented, as Shakespeare clearly intended, as a cautionary tale about the dangers of unbridled passion, whether the passion be hatred or an ill-conceived notion of love.

Wilfred Owen is, *me judice* and begging to differ with my younger self, one of the greatest poets ever to grace the English language. I have taught his poetry for years at the college level. Even so, he is very negative not merely about the war, on which his spleen was justifiably vented, but about everything else, almost to a nihilistic degree, and I always make a point of balancing his perspective alongside the poetry of Rupert Brooke and Siegfried Sassoon. My classmates and I would also have benefited from such balance, preserving us from the somewhat jaundiced perspective of life and love, as well as war, which Owen instills in the reader.

My naïve criticism of Orwell's fable is less tenable because the allegory at the heart of *Animal Farm* is far more applicable to the tyranny of Soviet communism, to which it clearly and implicitly alludes, than to fascism. Again, however, we were taught the book in dishonest fashion, our teacher implying that it was primarily an attack on Hitler. I was not, therefore, attacking *Animal Farm* for what it truly is as a great and timeless work of anti-communist literature, I was attacking the phantom of falsehood about the book that had been taught to me.

As for Wesker's play, its being set in the East End, with members of a Jewish socialist family as the protagonists, and with Oswald Mosley's Blackshirts* as the demonized enemy, was bound to be seen as a red rag to a bull to the bullishly belligerent person I had become. *Chicken Soup with Barley* was obviously nothing but crude communist propaganda and I condemned it as such. Today, I would not be so harsh. It was and is, however, a relatively obscure and minor work and one wonders why it warranted a place on the syllabus ahead of the numerous great works of literature which could have been selected instead. The fact that it was selected ahead of Austen, or Dickens, or Dostoyevsky, or Solzhenitsyn, to name but an illustrious few, suggests that a political motivation was indeed at work.

As the published article demonstrated, I had become utterly disillusioned with the education being offered to me and was openly hostile to the perceived political bias of my teachers. I showed my contempt by failing to attend classes, playing truant regularly, and by paying scant regard to my studies. The one solitary redeeming feature of my

---

* The British Union of Fascists, of which Sir Oswald Mosley was the leader.

school, or so I thought, was its choice of motto. Emblazoned in large letters above the stage of the school's auditorium were the words: "*This above all: To thine own self be true.*" —*William Shakespeare.* If I could take nothing else with me from my experience at Eastbury comprehensive school, I could at lease adopt and embrace the school's motto as my own. Throughout my life, above all else, I would be true to myself. Who could doubt the veracity of such a philosophy of life? Hadn't the great Shakespeare proclaimed it himself from the rooftops?

Once again, with the wisdom of hindsight, I can perceive the foolishness of the motto and the folly of adopting it as my own. The words are, of course, not Shakespeare's —at least, not exactly. They are uttered by Polonius as part of his famous advice to his son Laertes in *Hamlet.* Polonius' short speech as Laertes prepares to leave for Paris constitutes not only the father's advice to his son but the father's philosophy of life, which is utilitarian, irreligious, and radically relativistic. It contains practical advice on how to prosper in life, none of which is rooted in objective morality. The fact that Polonius is portrayed in a negative light and that his philosophy of relativism leads to his own violent death, the violent death of his son, and the madness and death of his daughter, serves as Shakespeare's own scathing indictment of relativism. This is obvious perhaps, but not, so it seems, to those who selected Polonius's words as the motto of my alma mater. Showing their ignorance of Shakespeare, the learned elders of Eastbury school had chosen the words of a blithering idiot as the epitome of the philosophy that the school sought to convey.

In the modern vernacular and in the spirit of the swinging sixties, being true to thyself could be translated as doing your own thing, something that most of my teachers happily encouraged. One of my teachers, an attractive dark-haired beauty, being true to herself and doing her own thing, had posed naked for a pornographic magazine during my time as a student, thereby showing her adherence to the noble tenets of the school motto and simultaneously causing something of a stir amongst her male adolescent students.

The problem, of course, is that relativism comes in many shapes and sizes, and emerges in many forms. Whereas one of my teachers was an avowed Marxist and another a naked exhibitionist, I also sought to be true to myself, above all else, which meant becoming a neo-fascist and white supremacist willing to lay down my life for my race and nation. I can understand how being true to myself can be condemned morally from the perspective of objective morality but I can't see how my truth, truthfully espoused and acted upon, is any less valid from the perspective of the relativism of my school's motto than choosing to become a Marxist class warrior or a model for pornographic magazines. If we are not meant to condemn others for doing their own thing, why should I be condemned for doing mine? This, it seems to me, is but one of the many problems attached to the relativist creed.

In any event, and returning to the journey upon which we are travelling, I was about to embark on a racist roller-coaster ride, full of thrills and dangers, and ups and downs, which would lead me a few years later to prison.

CHAPTER 6

WHITE RIOT

White riot — I wanna riot
White riot — a riot of my own
White riot — I wanna riot
White riot — a riot of my own

"White Riot" by the Clash (1977)

IN 1975, at the age of fourteen, I began to dabble in politics. By the following year it would completely dominate my life. The National Front (NF), a new political party founded eight years earlier, was growing in popularity, particularly in white working class areas. Two years later, the NF would gain 9 percent of the vote in Barking, the electoral constituency in which I lived, and would receive almost 20 percent of the vote in nearby Tower Hamlets. I began to scrawl swastikas and the National Front logo on walls and on my school books, and I was given the cane* when caught red-handed carving the NF logo into a wall with a knife. I also remember writing "Colin Jordan for

* Corporal punishment administered at school. It involved the culprit being struck once or several times with a flexible cane across the hand or buttocks.

PM; Charles Bond for MP"* on my school books. Charles Bond had been the NF candidate for Barking in the previous election and I was under the mistaken impression that Colin Jordan was the National Front's leader, whereas, in fact, he was not a member of the NF but the founder of the neo-Nazi National Socialist Movement.

Ironically, my racism did not prevent me from befriending the only Pakistani boy in my class. I recall going to his home and experiencing a deep visceral reaction against the smell of oriental spices wafting from the kitchen. I would soon learn to love Indian food but at this stage the very smell of curry made me feel angry, my aversion being a knee-jerk response to the Pakistani and Indian immigrants with whom I associated it. In spite of the barriers that my prejudice was placing between me and my friend, we got on very well for a while. Specific details of the friendship elude me but I do recall his showing me pornographic magazines. Inevitably my emerging racism meant that the friendship did not last, though I'm not aware of any rancor existing between us. We simply drifted apart. He was my first non-white friend and my only one for many years thereafter.

There is an intriguing and alarming post script to this friendship. About thirty years later, after my conversion and following my move to the United States, I was returning home to visit my parents in Barking. As I waited for a tube at Mile End station, two Pakistani men approached me and one of them asked me if I was "Joe Pearce." I didn't know them and presumed that they recognized me from

* i.e., Prime Minister and Member of Parliament respectively.

my political days when my photograph was in the newspapers and on television. I answered in the affirmative, somewhat cagily, expecting that they would react with anger or even violence to the confirmation that they were speaking to a notorious racist. To my surprise and relief, the man who had asked me my name did not look the least bit angry. He simply asked me if I remembered him. I was confused. I didn't know any Pakistanis. He then told me his name. It was my old friend. We were now middle-aged men but the shared memories of our teenage friendship fused a brief renewal of the old bond between us. At this point, however, the conversation took a bizarre and unsettlingly surreal turn. Instead of chastising me for my racism, my friend indicated that we had much in common politically. Sensing my confusion, he explained that we were both anti-Zionists and shared a hatred for Israel and the Jews. My friend had become a radical Islamist, as apparently full of hatred as I had been in my younger days, and willing to forge an alliance even with neo-Nazis to fight the Israeli enemy. I was dumbstruck and greatly relieved when my train arrived, providing an escape route from the situation in which I found myself.

This conversion of my old friend from adolescent hedonism to Islamic radicalism has caused a good deal of soul searching on my part. It shows the radicalizing of the Muslim community in the past thirty years and the consequent balkanization of British culture into warring sub-cultures. This is tragic. But is it more tragic than the triumph of hedonism? Would my Pakistani friend be happier, or a better person, if he had spent a life of self-gratification, addicted to the demands of his lower passions? Are pornography, prostitution, and abortion better and more liberating options than Islam? Should I be sad for my friend that he has become so embittered, or pleased that he has rejected the meretricious zeitgeist? In an ideal world I would have liked to have discussed religion and not politics with him. I would have liked to have discussed my conversion to Catholicism and to have asked him to explain his path from hedonism to religious conversion. Unfortunately we do not live in an ideal world and I suspect that such a discussion would have led to us departing in enmity not in friendship.

In spite of my erstwhile friendship with the son of Pakistani immigrants, I had soon adopted a violent approach to politics. The summer of 1976 was hot and humid, one of the hottest and longest on record. The heat seemed to raise the temperature of the passions as well as the body as racial violence throughout Britain reached record levels. I had joined the National Front in May of that year, lying about my age in order to do so because, at fifteen, I was a year too young for membership. My photograph appeared in the local paper on my first NF paper sale in Barking town centre and to this day I remember the look of fanatical anger on my face. I had metamorphosed into a political extremist.

In the long hot evenings, various gangs of white youths prowled the streets looking for isolated Sikhs or Muslims to attack. One of the local gangs was said to dress in SS uniform and would shoot any non-whites they came across with air pistols. Another local gang, the Dagenham Axe

Klan, the members of which I got to know well, were sort of Nazi hippies who would listen to music by Hawkwind and Frank Zappa and get high on LSD, before setting out on nights of psychedelic and psychopathic violence against hapless immigrants. Air rifles and stones were used repeatedly to smash the windows of the local Sikh temple as the war of attrition against the immigrant community spread.

My father's chivalrous approach to fighting saved me from the desire to join such gangs. The thought of being part of a gang of people kicking a defenseless person senseless filled me with revulsion and yet, perversely, I was pleased that the gangs existed and that they were doing their bit to stretch race relations to breaking point. The gang violence was dirty-work, in which I had no desire to involve myself, but it was dirty-work that needed doing for the good of the cause of race and nation. There was no making of an omelet without the cracking of eggs, and no making of a racially pure Britain without the cracking of skulls.

Although I did not involve myself in the Paki-bashing, as it was called, I found more than my share of violence on the National Front activities which I joined. There had long been a record of violence at National Front activities, though it must be said that the trouble was instigated by Marxist counter-demonstrators who sought to prevent the NF from holding its marches and meetings. In 1974, two years before I joined the Party, a young student, Kevin Gately, had been killed when taking part in a Marxist-organized violent counter-demonstration against a National Front meeting in Red Lion Square, in central London. He was only twenty-years-old and was the first person to be killed during a political demonstration in Britain for more than half a century. The Marxist left sought to make a martyr of Gately, whereas my NF comrades gloated over his death, singing that "Kevin Gately's body lies a-mouldering in the grave" to the tune of "Mine Eyes Have Seen the Glory."

Violence seemed to be woven into the very fabric of life for active members of the NF. On a local level, it was usual for National Front paper sellers to brawl with members of the Socialist Workers Party (SWP) as the two factions sought to sell their respective party's newspapers on the same busy streets. The enmity and hatred that existed between the members of the two groups precluded any possibility of agreeing to share the same street corners. On one occasion I wielded the flag pole I was holding as a weapon, breaking it across the torso of a rival paper seller. On another occasion I was embroiled in a street-fight between rival gangs of punk rockers and teddy boys*, though I can't

---

* Americans might not be familiar with teddy boys, a British youth cult, originally from the 1950s, which was associated with the first wave of rock n roll music. There was a teddy boy revival in the 1970s and the teds, as they were called colloquially, were sworn enemies of the punks, the latter of whom scorned the teds as conservative retrograde reactionaries and enemies of the new wave and the avant garde. Teddy boys were also associated with racism and were involved in race riots against Jamaican immigrants in the 1950s, whereas punks affirmed anarchy and nihilism as their political creed. It is worth remembering that youth cults in Britain were politically-charged during the 1970s and '80s, denoting not merely one's choice of music but one's political affiliations.

remember how I became involved. Having fought with the teddy boys, helping them defeat their rivals, I enlisted them to join me in an attack on the local SWP paper sellers up the road.

The endemic political violence at the local level was magnified manifold at the national marches and other activities, at which several thousand NF supporters would clash with several thousand Marxist counter-demonstrators, with thousands of police in the middle striving, not always successfully, to keep the rival mobs apart. The worst violence since the aforementioned Red Lion Square riots occurred at the National Front's annual St. George's Day march at Turnpike Lane in north London in April 1977. I travelled by tube with members of the Barking branch of the National Front to Turnpike Lane tube station. As we reached the top of the escalator a fight broke out between rival groups and a knife was pulled, though I don't remember anyone being stabbed. In order to get to where the National Front marchers were gathering we had to cross an open space of parkland. As we did so, a mob of Marxists spotted us and came charging towards us. We were greatly outnumbered but stood our ground, raising our arms in outstretched Nazi salutes as a mark of defiance while the mob descended upon us. As if by magic, or so it seemed to me at the time, the mob, which surely must have prevailed if it had continued with its rush towards us, stopped about twenty yards away, nobody wishing to be the first to take the plunge into the breach. Realizing that the wave had been broken upon the sheer chutzpah of our seemingly fearless defiance, we made contemptuous gestures towards our would-be assailants and proceeded to our destination. I am uneasy at the apparent boastfulness of these accounts of derring-do in the service of an unworthy cause but honesty seems to impel me to retell the events as I remember them.

At around the same time as the violence at Turnpike Lane, or perhaps even a little earlier, I was part of a smaller march, organized by the East London region of the NF, against the proposed building of a mosque in Leyton. As we assembled, it was clear that we were heavily outnumbered by a large group of vociferous counterdemonstrators further down the street. We were only a few dozen in number and the small contingent of police seemed entirely inadequate as a force capable of keeping the warring factions apart. It felt as though we were about to march to our deaths, or at least to serious injury. I found inspiration from the heroism of the Light Brigade, as recounted in the Tennyson poem that my father was in the habit of reciting when I was a child, and also from the speeches of Henry V in Shakespeare's imagined preludes to the battles of Harfleur and Agincourt. At the same time, the image of Horst Wessel, the Nazi martyr, murdered by a communist when he was only twenty-two-years-old, rose like a phoenix and lit a torch of courage, driving away the last vestiges of fear. As a true fanatic, I was ready to die a martyr's death for the cause. I marched off with my comrades, carrying a Union Flag towards the baying mob of counterdemonstrators. Marching past the Marxists it felt as though we were indeed, like the Light Brigade, entering into the valley of death. Yet we emerged unscathed, the police cordon holding back our enemies. We marched several times around the block where the mosque was going to be built, passing the counterdemonstrators each time. In the interim, our numbers grew ever larger as the people of the neighborhood joined our protest and I believe that we outnumbered the counterdemonstrators in the end. It was an indication of the depth of anger and resentment that mass immigration and the consequent rise of Islam was causing amongst the indigenous population of East London.

The violence at Turnpike Lane, the worst that I'd experienced thus far, was dwarfed by the violence that erupted in south-east London later in 1977 in what became known as the Battle of Lewisham. Racial tension had been rising in this area of London since a dawn raid on May 30 in which the police arrested around twenty people, all of them black, in connection with a spate of muggings in the area. The police claimed that the gang was responsible for most of the street crime in south-east London in the previous months. Two days later, as the gang members appeared in court, they fought with police in the courtroom, urged on by their supporters in the public gallery. A month later, as tensions surrounding the mass arrest of the suspected muggers continued to grow, a demonstration in their support, focusing on the alleged racism of the police, was held. I was part of a group of several hundred National Front activists who attacked this anti-police demonstration and was among the dozens arrested during the ensuing fracas. It was the first time that I'd ever been arrested, and I was furious that the police had arrested me for demonstrating in their support. In retrospect it seems absurd that I expected to use such violence under the noses of the police without suffering the legal consequences. Nonetheless, I believed then, and still suspect now, that the mass arrest of dozens of NF members was part of a police strategy, in the wake of the criticism that surrounded the arrest of the twenty suspected muggers, to show the police's impartiality and to deflect the charges of racism that had been directed against them. This was certainly the opinion of the National Front's leadership who, in retaliation for the arrests of its own members, announced that the NF would be holding a march through Lewisham in the following month. The date of the march was set for August 13. The Socialist Workers Party and other Marxist groups immediately announced their intention to stop the NF from marching, using whatever force necessary. The stage was set for what would be the worst political riot in England since the infamous Battle of Cable Street in 1936 at which a violent demonstration organized by the Communist Party succeeded in preventing a march through London's East End by the British Union of Fascists.

In the days and weeks before the proposed march, the national media focused on the rising tension and showed images of local residents and business owners boarding up their homes, offices, and shops in the expectation of the impending riot. Knowing that I would be present at the march and fearing for my safety, my father decided to come with me in the naïve though noble intention of protecting me. He was now forty-seven years-old. I was sixteen.

The actual events of the day are now something of a blur. The first thing I noticed upon my arrival at the assembly point was how different this particular NF march looked from the other ones I'd been on. On the previous marches, a substantial portion of those in attendance were middle-aged and elderly people, including many veterans from the Second World War. Many of these had stayed away, no doubt fearing the likely violence and feeling that their fighting days were over. In their place were hundreds of young people, many of them football hooligans, who were as attracted by the prospect of violence as the older NF supporters had been deterred by it. There was also a smattering of skinheads on the march, though the skinhead revival had not yet fully taken off. This was a sign of things to come. In the future, the older, respectable NF supporters, including the old soldiers, would stay away and fade away. In their place a younger, aggressive organization of young thugs would rise to become self-styled storm troopers of the New Order.

All hell broke loose as the NF march passed by the street on which the police had cordoned off the thousands of counterdemonstrators. At first we were showered with bricks, bottles, and other missiles hurled by our opponents. Then, as the rear of the NF march, of which I was a part, passed by our rioting opponents, the counterdemonstrators broke through the police lines and a wave of anger and hatred hit our ranks. I threw punches at my opponents and was punched in turn. The following moments are a frenzied haze. The assailing mob succeeded in pulling down the Barking Branch banner, behind which I had been marching, and as they pulled one of the banner poles into their own ranks I was caught behind it and dragged into the very midst of my rioting enemies. I was wearing a

National Front t-shirt emblazoned with a large union flag , identifying which side I was on, and now I was surrounded on all sides by an angry mob intent on beating me and my comrades senseless. If I had been spotted in their midst, I have no doubt that I would have been beaten to death. I was saved by the grace of God and by the manic confusion of the moment. Everyone around me was determined to get at the NF marchers, which was of course my intention also, though for very different reasons! I was, therefore, facing the same way as those who were attacking the march which meant that the union flag on the front of my shirt could not be seen from behind. Apparently part of the assailing mob and struggling more frantically than others to get at the NF marchers, I managed to fight my way back into the ranks of my own side. Curiously I don't recall feeling any fear in the midst of the fray, due perhaps to the fact that, in the heat of the moment, I did not have time to think of anything but my own survival.

Feeling exhilarated at what we perceived to be a great victory, we reached the place at which the concluding rally was held. I cheered with my comrades as several of the Party's leaders gave defiant and triumphalist speeches and then, escorted by the police, we left the area. Long after we had returned home, the counterdemonstrators were still rioting in the streets, attacking the police, and looting shops. More than two hundred people were arrested on that day and more than a hundred were injured. My father was astonished that nobody was killed.

CHAPTER 7

INCITING RACIAL HATRED

WITHIN a few weeks of the Battle of Lewisham I launched *Bulldog*, a youth magazine that was destined to change my life in dramatic fashion. The first issue was published in September 1977 by my local branch of the National Front. It was a one-man operation—or, considering that I was still only sixteen, a one-boy operation—because I was the magazine's editor and also the writer of all the articles.

Since *Bulldog* was aimed specifically at young people we started handing it out to students as they left local high schools. An explosion of outrage resulted. The news spread quickly and I was besieged by national television and newspaper reporters wanting to cover the story about the National Front's new plan to poison the minds of children. My comrades and I were filmed handing out *Bulldog* at school gates. I was interviewed widely, as were concerned headmasters and community leaders. The story made the national headlines. I was vilified as a racist and neo-Nazi and a corrupter of the minds of innocent children. I was angered at what I perceived as the one-sided bias of the news coverage, but I adhered to the belief that all publicity was good publicity. Indeed, looking back at the uproar across the chasm of the years, I am reminded of Oscar Wilde's famous quip that the only thing worse than being talked about is not being talked about. Although I no longer subscribe to such an outlook, it was certainly my belief in those heady days that there was no such thing as bad publicity. The immediate result of the national news coverage was that I began to receive bulk orders for *Bulldog* from National Front branches all over the country. By the beginning of 1978, the circulation of the magazine had increased ten-fold, from several hundred copies per issue to several thousand.

At the time of the publicity I was a student at South Bank Polytechnic,* having left high school a few months earlier.† A demonstration was held at the college at which several dozen students listened to speeches demanding that I be expelled. As a means of garnering extra publicity, I decided to attend the protest meeting in person under the pretext of free speech and demanded the right to defend myself. I was screamed at, spat upon, and assaulted with an umbrella by a black female student. In a few short weeks, I had become one of the most widely known members of the National Front and in January 1978, as a reward for my labors, I began to work for the Party in a fulltime capacity. I was now living every young radical's dream of being a fully paid, fulltime revolutionary, giving his life to the Cause.

I modeled *Bulldog* on the lowbrow tabloid press, keeping the articles short and direct, and always with an angry

---

* Now known as London South Bank University

† In Britain students could graduate from high school at sixteen.

teenage readership in mind. This made the content highly offensive to all but the most racist of readers. I started the "*Bulldog* Black List," encouraging school students to send details of so-called "red teachers." I published not only the teachers' names but also their addresses and phone numbers. Several teachers complained in the media of receiving threatening phone calls and offensive materials in the mail and, on at least one occasion, of being assaulted in the classroom. *Bulldog* also initiated the "Racist League," which encouraged football hooligans to send in reports of racist abuse and racist chants at soccer games. Fans of rival teams sought to outdo each other and become top of the league. Fans of Chelsea, Leeds, West Ham, and Newcastle were amongst the most racist.

Although I would deny the charges in court, it would be true to say that *Bulldog*'s ultimate purpose was to incite racial hatred. The strategy was simple. We had to stir up enmity and hatred between black and white youths, thereby making multiracialism untenable and a race war inevitable. The newly formed Young National Front, of which I was soon elected chairman, would become an army of race warriors, a new *Sturmabteilung*,* the stormtroopers of the New Order. The strategy was actually identical with Trotskyism. The only difference was that Trotskyites, such as our sworn enemies in the Socialist Workers Party, sought to incite class hatred in order to bring about a class war while we endeavored to incite racial hatred to bring about a race war.

---

* The notorious "Storm Section" or stormtroopers of Hitler's Nazi Party, sometimes known as the brownshirts.

As *Bulldog* continued to grow, I became more popular as a speaker at National Front meetings up and down the country. On St. George's Day 1979 I was one of the speakers at a National Front election meeting in Southall, a town in Middlesex, on the western edge of London, close to Heathrow airport, which had the largest Indian population in London. They were mostly Sikhs but there were also many Muslims and Hindus. Today almost 90 percent of Southall's population is non-white. Clearly a National Front election meeting in such a racially sensitive and potentially volatile area was considered an act of the grossest provocation on the NF's part, which indubitably it was. Nonetheless, the NF's position was that it had a candidate standing for election in the area and that he and his supporters had a democratic right to campaign for votes.

The Socialist Workers Party and other militant Marxist groups, including the newly formed Anti-Nazi League, agitated for the NF meeting to be banned, threatening to mobilize a mob from across the country to descend upon Southall if a ban was not enforced. There were, in fact, no grounds in law to ban the meeting because British electoral law enshrined the democratic right of candidates to organize meetings during elections. Once again the scene was set for another almighty riot.

On the scheduled day, I was shuttled to Southall town hall, the location for the meeting, with a large police escort. As I gave my speech I could hear a riot outside the building. Before it was brought under control, more than forty people had been injured, half of them policemen, and three hundred people had been arrested. Tragically one of the protesters, Blair Peach, an active and longtime member of the Socialist Workers Party, was killed.

Racial tensions were higher than ever in England, exacerbated by the efforts of both extremes, the National Front and the Socialist Worker Party, to fan the flames of hatred for their own revolutionary political ends. This tension erupted into renewed and even worse violence in April 1981 as the West Indian community in Brixton in south London rioted against the police. During two days of anarchy, nearly three hundred police officers and around fifty rioters were injured. More than a hundred vehicles were set on fire, half of them police vehicles. Almost one hundred and fifty buildings were damaged in an orgy of looting, thirty of which were burned to the ground.

I was living in nearby Herne Hill at the time, only a mile from the epicenter of the violence. Rather recklessly, I decided to go and see the riots for myself, reveling in the further unraveling of the multi-racial society. The flames from burning buildings and from petrol bombs lit the night sky as I watched the black community unleash its fury against the police. Occasionally the lines of police, wielding riot shields, would advance upon the crowd and I found myself on more than one occasion retreating with the mob. The irony of my presence amongst the rioters added a grim and gruesome humor to the surreal scenario. Suddenly police snatch squads* raced towards the crowd wielding batons and intent on making arrests. I fled with

* Small groups of police officers trained to rush at rioters to make arrests, after which they would retreat with the arrested rioters behind police lines, protected by the riot shields of their colleagues.

the scattering mob, the police in hot pursuit. Suddenly it dawned on me that I was in a very dangerous position. Were I to be arrested, it would be reported in the press that a leading member of the National Front was present amongst the rioters. I had visions of being framed as an *agent provocateur* stirring the mob into a frenzy and becoming a scapegoat on whom the events could be blamed. Perhaps my fears were a little far-fetched but they were real enough to induce me to leave the scene hastily and return to the safety of my own home.

During this whole period I had been brazenly daring the Director of Public Prosecutions, the government's chief prosecutor, to charge me with offences under the Race Relations Act for my editorship of *Bulldog*. This act, hated by racists as an infringement of their civil liberties, made it illegal to publish material likely to incite racial hatred. In the name of free speech, I published articles that were deliberately provocative and offensive in the hope of provoking the government to prosecute me for a "hate crime." A few years earlier, in 1976, the government had made itself unpopular with a large section of the population by prosecuting Robert Relf under the Race Relations Act for putting up a sign outside his house advertising it for sale "to an English family only." He was sent to prison for contempt of court when he refused to comply with a court order to take the sign down. Knowing that the Race Relations Act was unpopular, the government seemed reluctant to enforce it. My stance was designed, therefore, as a Mexican stand-off. If the government refused to take the bait, however offensive, it indicated that the Race Act was effectively dead, if not buried, because of the unwillingness of the government to wield its power to enforce the act. On the other hand, if the Director of Public Prosecutions took the bait and brought charges against me, it was hoped that the action would prove as unpopular with the public as had the earlier prosecution of Robert Relf, thereby winning support for the National Front.

Eventually, in 1981, the DPP took the bait, or called my bluff. I was duly charged with publishing material likely to incite racial hatred and was tried at the Old Bailey to the accompaniment of national media coverage. The barrister who defended me made the right to free speech a major part of his case, quoting the famous maxim attributed to Voltaire: "I disapprove of what you say but I will defend to the death your right to say it." He concluded his summing up to the jury by suggesting that mine was a rather small and largely insignificant voice, if perhaps an eccentric and ugly one, and that the use of the Race Relations Act to silence me was like taking a huge sledgehammer to crack a tiny nut. Although the double-entendre implied in the use of the word "nut" was not flattering to me, it raised the desired smile among some members of the jury. His line of reasoning proved persuasive to at least several jury members because the jury as a whole could not reach a verdict.

I left the court a free man, emerging into the street to the cheers of a crowd of supporters who sensed that a great victory had been won. The victory would be short-lived. A few months later I would be re-tried on the same charges, found guilty on a majority verdict, and sentenced to six months in prison.

CHAPTER 8

PORTRAIT OF A FRIEND

AT THIS juncture it is necessary to backtrack several years to pick up several threads that need to be woven into the fabric of the story.

At around the same time that *Bulldog* was making the headlines, I was invited to the inaugural meeting of the Young National Front, which was held at the NF's regional headquarters in Leicester. Young members of the Party from all over Britain were in attendance, and it was here that I first met Nick Griffin, who is now the leader of the British National Party and a Member of the European Parliament. Nick and I, along with six or seven others, were elected to the governing body of the newly formed YNF, under the watchful eye of its first chairman, Andrew Fountaine, a stentorian figure whose silver-spooned and plum-mouthed accent reflected his blue-blooded roots in the landed gentry.

Fountaine was an interesting character. He was only in his late-fifties when I first met him but to my teenage eyes he seemed much older. He resided in the stately splendor of Narford Hall, which had been built by his ancestor, also named Andrew Fountaine, in the early eighteenth century on the family's estate near the Norfolk market town of Swaffham. As an adventurous teenager, he had gone to Spain to fight for Franco's Nationalist forces in the Spanish Civil War—a quixotic gesture that commanded respect—and then became a Lieutenant Commander in the Royal Navy during the Second World War. I heard that he had earned the dubious distinction of being the last officer in the Navy to order his men to be flogged, more than sixty years after the practice had been officially abolished, and that he had been severely reprimanded for doing so. In fairness, I have not verified this fact, which was one of the many stories circulated about this most eccentric of figures during my days of involvement with him. He was an imposing figure, cigar in hand, and we were all convinced that he was slightly mad. We were greatly relieved when he was replaced as chairman of the Young National Front by a gentle and mild-mannered lawyer. Soon after, I became the YNF's Chairman, affording me much more freedom to do as I willed with an organization that was burgeoning in size.

Considering how famous—or infamous—Nick Griffin has become in recent years, due to the electoral successes of the British National Party, it would be well if I were to say something about my friendship with him. We became the best of friends and I gained much from our relationship. My visits to Hill House, his parents' home in Suffolk, made a lasting and positive impact upon me. The Griffins lived in an isolated and rustic farmhouse with uneven wooden floors, low beams and old-fashioned latched doors to all the rooms. They cooked on a woodburning stove, which also heated the whole house. The food was always so much better than the instant and tinned food with which I was familiar, igniting my taste buds and my consciousness to the superiority of traditional and natural food, a passion and predilection for the good things in life which has stayed with me and has grown in the subsequent years. The smell of bread baking in their oven wafts across the years to me as mouthwateringly as ever and the piquance of the farmhouse cheddar, so splendid and so superior to anything I had ever tasted before, dances on my tongue's memory to the melancholy melody of days long gone.

Lest such poetic dalliance seems a little out of place, I can only insist that my experience of visiting the Griffin family home awakened a poetic and romantic sensibility in me which had been largely dormant until then. It was an awakening to a fuller and better vision of the beauty of life, particularly country life, to which I had been largely unaware until then. Perhaps it had something to do with a rekindling of my own happy childhood in the Shire, which would be natural enough considering that the Griffins lived in Suffolk, the same county in which I'd spent my carefree early years, though the Griffins lived in the east of the county, about forty miles from my former home in Haverhill. In any event, I find it impossible to write honestly and earnestly about my visits to Hill House prosaically. The sheer hominess of the place was accentuated by the presence of Nick's doddering old grandfather, who was around ninety-years-old and looked positively ancient as he pottered about the house and busied himself in the garden. He seemed to belong in a bygone, magical age.

It was also at Hill House that I first experienced the magical presence of starlight. Prior to that I had only seen stars through the obscuring and polluting presence of artificial street-lighting. If I had been in the presence of clear and clean starlight during my childhood I had no reminiscence of it, an indication that I had been too young to notice or care about such splendor at the time.

I remember one night in particular when Nick and I decided to go to the local pub, the Huntingfield Arms, which was about a mile away and which was also, I think, the nearest neighboring building. As we stepped out of the house into the night and began ambling down the country lane, I was struck by how pitch-black it all seemed. I could hardly see anything in front of me and began to doubt the wisdom of groping our way for a whole mile in such conditions. Slowly my eyes adjusted and the dark outlines of trees and hedgerows emerged. Above us were more stars than I had ever seen, more than I had ever thought could be seen. It was a dazzling display of pins of light pricking the darkness and it seemed as though my eyes were being caressed by the "moth-soft Milky Way," to borrow a phrase from Hopkins. Having my eyes awakened to such beauty was a baptism of the imagination—a baptism of desire—which I now see as foundational to my path to religious conversion.

It must have been a moonless night, considering how dark it had been, in spite of the stars. My first experience of walking in the countryside by the light of a full moon, casting such bright shadows that it almost seemed like day, would happen a few years later on New Year's Eve as I walked across fields after leaving a pub near Dedham, on the border of Suffolk and Essex, an area of England made famous by the artist John Constable.

I must insist that this aesthetic digression is not irrelevant to the journey from racial hatred to rational love. One must realize and acknowledge the apparent contradictions and incongruities in the minds and hearts of men if one is to understand them. I am reminded again of my father's deep love for people in spite of his racial and tribal prejudices. I am reminded also that my own descent into the nasty world of racial hatred was not motivated primarily by hatred but by a disordered and perverted love for my own country and people. The animus of the political creed to which I subscribed was not animosity towards aliens but a love of my own people, albeit a love that became an idol, a false god that I worshipped at the expense of my own spiritual wellbeing. In similar vein, a love of beauty, once awakened in me, was a light that shone in the inner darkness of my soul, leading me to a light of which I was unaware.

Thus far, the description of my friendship with Nick Griffin has centered on his family and their home in the countryside. Now I should turn to Nick himself.

An important influence that Nick had on me in those early days was his engagement with history, which enabled me to see beyond the narrow vista of history that I had inherited from my father. Nick had been an enthusiastic member of the Sealed Knot, a battle re-enactment society which focused on the English Civil War. From such gatherings, he had learned many English folk songs, which he and I and our comrades would sing around camp fires, especially during gatherings at his parents' home. He also lent me a long-playing record of songs of the British Red Coats, which (mea culpa!) I never returned to him. More importantly, he introduced me to the writing and thought of John Seymour, who would become a major beneficial influence, and, I believe, to Schumacher's *Small is Beautiful*, to which we shall return presently.

In late 1979 or early 1980 Nick's rooms at Downing College in Cambridge, where he was in his final year as an undergraduate studying law, was the venue for a secret meeting to discuss plans for a new magazine, *Nationalism Today*, the first issue of which would be published in April 1980. The meeting was secret because of the internecine disputes that were dividing the nationalist movement at the time and which would lead to the fragmentation of the National Front and the eventual emergence of the British National Party as the dominant force, of which Nick would eventually become leader. At the time, Nick and I were in the vanguard of a group of young radicals who had become disillusioned with the leadership of the NF and who sought new ideological paths. I became the editor of the new magazine, and Nick and I worked closely together on every issue for five years until another of the interminable internecine disputes drove a division between us.

On the day of Nick's graduation in the summer of 1980 I joined his family for a delightful picnic on the banks of the River Cam in the shadow of the Old Vicarage at Grantchester, which had been immortalized by the poet, Rupert Brooke, who lived there prior to the First World War:

Ah God! to see the branches stir
Across the moon at Grantchester!
To smell the thrilling-sweet and rotten
Unforgettable, unforgotten
River-smell, and hear the breeze
Sobbing in the little trees.
Say, do the elm-clumps greatly stand
Still guardians of that holy land?
The chestnuts shade, in reverend dream,
The yet unacademic stream? . . .
Oh, is the water sweet and cool,
Gentle and brown, above the pool?
And laughs the immortal river still
Under the mill, under the mill?
Say, is there Beauty yet to find?
And Certainty? and Quiet kind?
Deep meadows yet, for to forget
The lies, and truths, and pain? . . . oh! yet
Stands the Church clock at ten to three?
And is there honey still for tea?

The elegiac feel of Brooke's wistful yearning for Grantchester evokes my own memories, not only of the picnic with Nick's family but of our swimming in the river before dawn on the following morning, in a thunder storm, before setting off on a hike along the nearby Devil's Dyke.

Shortly after Nick's graduation we became neighbors when he moved to a house in Herne Hill, only a hundred yards or so from the house in which I was living at the time and from which I had made my ill-advised sortie to the

Brixton riots. It was at this time that I first met his girlfriend, Jackie. A few years later when they were married, I was honored to be Best Man at their wedding, the apogee and crowning moment of our friendship. Sadly, not so long afterwards, during my second prison sentence, our friendship was sundered by what I still believe to be an ignoble and ignominious act of betrayal on Nick's part of mutual friends of ours. More on this later.

The last time that Nick and I met was in 1990, a year or so after my reception into the Catholic Church and three years after I had dropped out of politics. I can't remember why he happened to be in Norwich, the city in which I was living at the time, but he visited me in the tiny apartment in which I was living and we had our last conversation. We were looking for common ground but an abyss now separated us. I tried to explain that action needed to be rooted in philosophical and theological first principles whereas he was still stuck on the level of ideology and day-to-day political struggle. From my vantage point, I was saddened to see that Nick had not progressed beyond the politics of our youth. He had ossified. I had moved on, progressed. He was where he had always been which was a place that I no longer wanted to be. I dare say that from his perspective I was the one who was blameworthy. He had remained true to the faith that we had both shared; I had lapsed into disbelief. He remained a true believer; I was an apostate. We departed the sadder for the meeting, knowing that the fire of faith and friendship we had once shared could not be rekindled.

In the light of the loss of such friendship, even if it is a loss that is paradoxically a gain, I can't help recalling some lines of Chesterton, not least because I am still in possession of Nick's own copy of Chesterton's *Orthodoxy*, given to me as a gift, perhaps, or lent to me and never returned:

> And I dream of the days when work was scrappy,
> And rare in our pockets the mark of the mint,
> When we were angry and poor and happy,
> And proud of seeing our names in print. *

I have deliberately entitled this chapter "Portrait of a Friend" in imitation of Chesterton's choice of that title for the chapter in his autobiography on his friendship with Belloc. Although Chesterton's friendship with Belloc was never sundered or sullied, as was mine with Nick, there is the same elegiac quality in Chesterton's chapter on his friend as there is in this chapter on my friend.

Chesterton ends his chapter on Belloc by borrowing lines by Sir William Watson:

> Nor without honour my days ran,
> Nor yet without a boast shall end;
> For I was Shakespeare's countryman
> And were not you my friend.†

---

* From "A Song of Defeat," G. K. Chesterton.

† Illustrating his habitual carelessness with regard to accuracy and betraying the fact that he was quoting from memory without consulting the source, Chesterton actually misquotes Watson's lines. The correct rendition of the lines from Watson's poem "To Richard Holt Hutton" is as follows: "And not uncrowned with honours ran / My days, and not without a boast shall end! / For I was Shakespeare's countryman / And wert not thou my friend?"

For my part, I shall conclude by borrowing lines from Belloc:

> From quiet homes and first beginning,
> Out to the undiscovered ends,
> There's nothing worth the wear of winning,
> But laughter and the love of friends.*

I have long since learned that there are other things worth the wear of winning than friendship and laughter, not least of which is joy and peace in the love of Christ. It is nonetheless true that laughter and friendships are a great source of comfort and consolation in this vale of tears. They should not be taken lightly and should be lamented when lost. Nick and I took different paths. Mine, I'm sure, is the better of the two. It is my parting wish, and thought, and prayer, that the gall of bitterness may be washed from Nick Griffin's heart and that the love of God and neighbor will rise like a new dawn in its place.

---

* From "Dedicatory Ode"

CHAPTER 9

RICHARD DAWKINS AND OTHER BAD INFLUENCES

AS DISCUSSED in an earlier chapter, I became a full time employee of the National Front in January 1978, shortly before my seventeenth birthday. Every morning and evening I made the two-hour commute, involving one bus and three trains, from my parents' home in Barking on the eastern edge of London to NF headquarters in Teddington, Middlesex, which was on the diametrically opposite western edge of the Greater London conurbation. Each day, therefore, I had four hours of reading time to indulge my insatiable bibliophilia. I spent it gorging myself on what purported to be the seminal works underpinning the NF's racial nationalist ideology.

One of the most popular books at the time amongst the NF's intelligentsia was *The Selfish Gene* by Richard Dawkins. I remember excited conversations in which Dawkins' ideas were used to justify racism, racial selection, and racial segregation, all of which, thanks to interpretations of Dawkins' arguments, were considered beneficial to the evolution of the species. Racism was in our genes and was, therefore, not only natural but was an inexorable and positive force in the process of Darwinian evolution. Dawkins' assertion that individuals who are closely related genetically will be predisposed or predetermined genetically to act altruistically towards each other was taken to its logical conclusion and applied to the races of man. Since people of the same race are more closely related genetically to each other than to members of other races it followed from Dawkins' principles that a sense of racial kinship and loyalty was genetically beneficial. It also followed that racial miscegenation was biologically regressive and an affront to the inherent progressivism of man's evolutionary ascent. It was a biological "sin" against omnipotent natural selection. On a more complex level, it was argued from Dawkins' assertion that populations are genetically wired towards an evolutionarily stable strategy that human races and nations, being predetermined by their respective gene pools, must also seek evolutionary stability by excluding alien genes from the population.

Taking Dawkins as their guru, the National Front's intelligentsia, especially in the pages of *New Nation*, which was launched in 1980, hailed the new science of sociobiology as providing irrefutable scientific justification for the NF's racial policies. The arguments of sociobiology that human behavior is determined genetically removed all the outmoded Christian moral arguments against racism, freeing racists to frame the debate on racial questions in a new amoral light, or even to claim that racism was "moral" due to its conformity with Darwinian presumptions about the human species and human society.

In addition to the apparent scientific justification that Richard Dawkins had provided for the NF's ideological stance on racial issues, the work of two psychologists, Hans Eysenck and Arthur Jenson, was also cited regularly to buttress the racist position. Building on the earlier work done by Jenson in the United States, Eysenck's *Race, Intelligence and Education* was considered compulsory reading for any young racist wishing to understand the intellectual basis for his beliefs, supplying what was considered irrefutable evidence of genetically determined differences in inherent intelligence between the races. Eysenck stated unequivocally that "[a]ll the evidence to date suggests the . . . overwhelming importance of genetic factors in producing the great variety of intellectual differences which we observe in our culture, and much of the difference observed between certain racial groups."*

Basing my arguments on "scientific evidence" such as this, I wrote the text of a flyer on racial differences which was distributed outside schools and which included a diagram of the skulls of a white man, a black man, and a chimpanzee, measuring the angle of the forehead of each to show that blacks were closer to chimpanzees than they were to whites.

Although the NF's position was always to deny strongly that it was a neo-Nazi party, one could not graduate to the inner-sanctum of the cognoscenti within the Party without tacitly accepting Nazi ideology and without secretly

---

* Hans Eysenck, *Race, Intelligence and Education*, London: Temple Smith, 1971, p. 130

regretting the defeat of Hitler and the Third Reich. As such, my education in racial nationalist ideology included a broad reading of essential Nazi "classics." I tried to read Hitler's *Mein Kampf* with the care and reverence that the Führer's magnum opus demanded but found the experience anti-climactic. It was not that I disagreed with anything that Hitler had written, it was simply that it was not very riveting reading. I read Mussolini's autobiography and was repelled by Il Duce's irrepressibly vulgar vanity. It cured me, once and for all, of any real devotion to the man, except for the respect due to him for defeating the hated communists. I read some of the speeches of Hitler's propaganda minister, Josef Goebbels, and found him much more appealing than the Führer. There was something utterly ruthless and uncompromising about him which was very attractive to the young racist zealot that I had become.

Used bookstores were a favorite haunt, and on one of my expeditions into these dens of discovery I came across a peculiar book published by Goebbels' Nazi propaganda ministry, which had been translated into English. It was entitled *Christianity in the Third Reich* or something of that sort and was written, if I remember correctly, by a German Protestant clergyman who was also a thoroughly committed Nazi. The book contained quotes from Scripture purporting to justify the Nazi Party and especially its anti-Semitism. I had this book on my shelf for years before selling it to a friend. I regret doing so. I suspect that, as a rare and singular example of Nazi propaganda in English, it is worth much more than I received for it and, in any case, it would have been interesting to re-read the book now that

I have a grasp of Scriptural theology which I lacked entirely when I had first read it.

Continuing my racial nationalist education, I struggled manfully but I think not altogether successfully with Oswald Spengler's *Decline of the West*, finding its pessimistic determinism a little off-putting, and I also tried reading, with no more success, Francis Parker Yockey's *Imperium*, which was written as a conscious sequel to Spengler's seminal work. Looking back on my failure to show Spengler and Yockey the respect that many of my comrades felt they deserved, I suspect that the reason is the lingering and lurking presence of Friedrich Nietzsche's influence on their work. Nietzsche was another figure held in high regard by the National Front's intellectual highbrows whom I always found uncongenial. I had not yet discovered the work of G. K. Chesterton but his criticism of Nietzschean and Spenglerian pessimism and especially its underlying determinism held the key to my own lack of sympathy with their ideas: "The pessimists believe that the cosmos is a clock that is running down; the progressives believe it is a clock that they themselves are winding up. But I happen to believe that the world is what we choose to make it, and that we are what we choose to make ourselves; and that our renascence or our ruin will alike, ultimately and equally, testify with a trumpet to our liberty."*

Alongside the National Front's duplicitous denial of its Nazi sympathies was its denial that it was anti-Semitic. The official Party line was that the NF was not anti-Semitic but

---

* *Illustrated London News*, July 10, 1920

anti-Zionist. In fact, however, crude anti-Semitism was rife and rampant in the Party, the more so the more one ascended the levels of its hierarchy. Amongst the elite coterie which comprised the Party's leadership anti-Semitism was worn as a badge of honor and seen as a de facto condition of membership. Finding myself at such a young age on the fringes of the leadership, it was natural that I should be directed to read the "classics" of anti-Semitism.

I read the notorious *Protocols of the Learned Elders of Zion* but was troubled by allegations that it was a literary forgery and not the genuine minutes of a meeting of Jewish conspirators plotting world domination. Seeking reassurance, I asked one of the Party's leaders whether the *Protocols* were an authentic and bona fide historical document or only an elaborate hoax. He admitted sheepishly that the document was probably a forgery but that nonetheless it retained its value as a work of prophecy of what the Jews are actually planning and doing in reality. I was not entirely happy or comfortable with this explanation but accepted it readily enough through a sense of duty and loyalty to the cause. One of the Nazi Party's greatest commentators on the *Protocols* was Alfred Rosenberg, whose anti-Semitic, racist, and anti-Christian ideas I imbibed with largely unreserved approval, though I found the shrill and pathological anti-Semitic rantings of Julius Streicher and his British acolyte Arnold Leese completely unsettling. (Ironically my elderly landlord when I lived in Herne Hill, Bert Wilton, was a former member of Leese's Imperial Fascist League. In spite of his anti-Semitism and dubious political connections he forged a successful career as a trumpeter in the big band era, playing with Jewish bandleaders Harry Roy and Stanley Black and being featured in *Melody Maker* as one of the country's finest trumpeters.)

A corollary of the NF's anti-Semitism was its enthusiastic support for those revisionist historians who were questioning the truth of the Holocaust. I read *The Hoax of the Twentieth Century* by Arthur R. Butz, which was sub-titled "the case against the presumed extermination of European Jewry," and a magazine format summary of Butz's main arguments entitled *Did Six Million Really Die?*, which was written pseudonymously by a member of the NF's Executive Council. I also read *The Destruction of Dresden* by David Irving with a feeling of anger that the Allies had been hypocritical in condemning Nazis for war crimes when they had also sanctioned the systematic extermination of civilians through the blanket bombing of German cities.

Other anti-Semitic works read during this period included *For My Legionaries*, the autobiography of Corneliu Codreanu, the charismatic leader of the Rumanian Iron Guard, who would become something of a cult figure amongst the young radical elements in the National Front, and *World Revolution* by Nesta Webster, which was subtitled, "The plot against civilization." I read the latter with engrossed fascination, submerging myself in the author's paranoid and self-delusional theories, woven into a febrile fabric of Jewish and Masonic conspiracy theories. This was one of the books I read on my long commute to NF headquarters in 1978, when I was only seventeen, so perhaps I can be forgiven for falling under Webster's spell. Others, much older and wiser than I, had been similarly beguiled. The book was the product of a series of lectures given to British army officers, including officers of the British secret service who had urged her to publish them. Amongst her outspoken admirers were Lord Kitchener and Winston Churchill, the latter of whom claimed in 1920 that Nesta Webster had "so ably shown . . . this worldwide conspiracy for the overthrow of civilisation."* Hilaire Belloc, whose works I had not yet discovered, was much more discerning. Writing of "a woman called Webster" to an American Jewish friend, Belloc dismissed her work in forthright terms:

> In my opinion it is a lunatic book. She is one of those people who have got one cause on the brain. It is the good old Jewish revolutionary bogey. I think people are great fools who do not appreciate what a part the Jew has played in revolutionary movements, but people are much bigger fools who get it on the brain and ascribe every revolutionary movement to Jews and secret societies. The prime cause of revolution is injustice, and the protest against injustice, when it becomes too violent, produces revolution. But there is a type of unstable mind which cannot rest without morbid imaginings, and the conception of single causes simplifies thought. With this good woman it is the Jews, with some people it is the Jesuits, with others Freemasons and so on. The

* Winston Churchill, "Zionism versus Bolshevism: A Struggle for the Soul of the Jewish People," published in the *Illustrated Sunday Herald* (London), February 8, 1920.

> world is more complex than that. Many of the facts quoted are true enough, but the inferences drawn are exaggerated.*

Having not thought about Nesta Webster's book for years, I had a flashback to its warnings about the sinister conspiracy of the secretive Illuminati when, in January 2009 at my mother's funeral, I was accused of being part of that very conspiracy myself! The bizarre accusation was sparked by anger at my Catholicism amongst some of my relatives. At the funeral and at the reception which followed it, I was wearing a small crucifix pin on my lapel, as is my custom, which was like a red rag to a bull to some of those present. One man, a friend of my brother, recoiling from the presence of the crucifix, pulled out a pentangle that he had been wearing around his neck as if to ward off the evil of the Cross with his occult magic. It was like one of those trashy 1950s horror films in which Dracula recoils from the Cross, except that the role was now comically reversed with the practitioner of the occult brandishing the magic symbol to ward off good spirits! In spite of this unpromising start, we fell into polite conversation. My pentangled friend told me that he kept three holy books by his bed at all times. One was the Bible, another was some work of Buddhism, the title of which escapes me, . . . and the third

---

* The letter was addressed to Major Louis Henry Cohn and dated February 6, 1924; quoted in Robert Speaight, *The Life of Hilaire Belloc*, New York: Farrar, Straus & Giroux, Inc., 1957, pp. 456-57. Belloc is actually referring to a different book by Webster but the critique applies equally to both books.

was *Mein Kampf* by Adolf Hitler! As my initial frown of consternation changed into a tight-lipped effort to stifle the desire to laugh, he assured me in all earnestness that all wisdom was to be found in one or other or a combination of these books.

Later, as more beer was imbibed, I was confronted by an apoplectic relative who screamed his hatred of the Church at me. He asked me if I had heard of the Illuminati, at which the flashback to my reading of Webster's *World Revolution* sprang to mind. Puzzled by the apparent irrelevance of the question, I replied that I was indeed familiar with it. Well, he retorted with a note of triumph, the Catholic Church was run by the Illuminati and was part of an evil fascist conspiracy. Suspecting that this particular person had never read a book in his life, I informed him that I had read several books about the Illuminati and asked him whether he had done likewise. He looked at me askance as if to ask what books had to do with it! This was, after all, the age of the internet and the History Channel. Who needs books? On the following day, en route from the madness of modern England to the relative sanity of South Carolina, I pondered the observation, often attributed to Chesterton, that when people stop believing in God, they don't believe in nothing but in anything.

This tragicomic aside illustrates the "type of unstable mind which cannot rest without morbid imaginings," and which turns to conspiracy theories as a means of simplifying thought to the level of the lowest common denominator, thereby excluding any knowledge of the complexity of reality or even the very desire for such knowledge. It is an escape from serious thought into the realm of self-delusional bigotry. This type was all too common in the National Front, fuelled by books such as Webster's but also by some of the other conspiracy-oriented books that I read at this time, including *The New Unhappy Lords* by A. K. Chesterton, a distant relative of the better-known (and better) Chesterton, which was considered required reading. Other books in similar vein which I devoured during my teenage years included *The Naked Capitalist* by W. Cleon Skousen and *None Dare Call It Conspiracy* by Gary Allen.

Although the dangers associated with conspiracy theorizing need emphasizing, it would be well to avoid falling into the opposite error of what might be termed accidentalism, the belief that everything happens because of impersonal forces and that conspiracies play no role at all in the manipulation of world events. A few contemporary examples of accidentalist fundamentalism are free market libertarianism, which ascribes quasi-mystical omnipotence to market forces; social progressivism, which ascribes similar omnipotence to the power of time and the mystical shadow of the future; and philosophical materialism, which ascribes absolute power to matter to the exclusion of the possibility of the existence of free will. The path of truth winds its way between the two extremes of conspiracism and accidentalism. On the one hand, only the most naïve, or those with something to hide, will deny that world events are manipulated by those in power and that dirty deeds are done behind closed doors; on the other, only the most foolish refuse to acknowledge the existence of powerful forces which limit the ability of such conspiracies to manipulate reality entirely in accordance with their own collective and conspiratorial will. As Belloc said, "the conception of single causes simplifies thought" and fails to see that "the world is more complex than that."

CHAPTER 10

THREE NOVELS AND A REAL-LIFE HERO

THE BRIEF survey of my youthful reading and its mainly negative influence should not exclude three novels that impacted me powerfully at this time. The three, taken together, could be called the good, the bad, and the ugly. The good novel was George Orwell's *Nineteen Eighty-four*. Recall that I had read Orwell's *Animal Farm* at school but was too young to really appreciate its anti-totalitarian message at the time. I read *Nineteen Eighty-four* at exactly the time that my intellect and imagination had ripened sufficiently for its fruitful reception. Its effect was to dampen my enthusiasm for totalitarianism and to plant the early seeds of libertarianism or what I would now prefer to call subsidiarism* into my political consciousness. From this time on, I began to see Big Government as synonymous with Big Brother, though as a member of the National Front I accepted that some form of Big Government would be

* A political philosophy rooted in the concept of subsidiarity as defined in the *Catechism of the Catholic Church*.

necessary to carry out the Party's policies. I was, therefore, guilty of Orwellian doublethink, though I didn't realize it at the time, believing that Big Government was bad except for the Big Government in which I believed. In the long term, such duplicity is untenable rationally and I would have to face the crux of the dilemma enunciated by the Catholic historian Lord Acton that power tends to corrupt and absolute power tends to corrupt absolutely. The reading of *Nineteen Eighty-four* led me in the direction of the dilemma and the clarity of the solution that would emerge in my confronting of it. For this reason, if for no other, I am indebted to George Orwell for his part in my conversion.

The one aspect of Orwell's novel which made me feel uneasy at the time, for all its dark and penetrating power, was the ultimate pessimism suggested in the crushing of the dissident Winston Smith and the triumph of Big Brother. I desired what Tolkien would call the consolation of the happy ending and was uncomfortable with Orwell's portrayal of the victory of evil.

The bad novel in the trio of titles that I read in the late 1970s was *The Turner Diaries* by Andrew Macdonald, a pseudonym for William Pierce, leader of the American white supremacist organization, the National Alliance. This was a lowbrow thriller in which white rebels emerge victorious in a race war. It was easy to read and well-written in the mode of populist pulp fiction—a page-turner* in popular parlance—but I found its salacious indulgence of bloodthirsty barbarism distasteful. Considering how angry,

* The pun on the novel's title is unintentional!

embittered, and racist I was in those days the fact that *The Turner Diaries* still assaulted my residual civilized sensibility will give some indication of exactly how outrageously racist and violent it was.

The ugly novel in the trio was *The Camp of the Saints* by Jean Raspail, a true classic of twentieth century literature which would be more widely known were it not for its racism and political incorrectness. I call it ugly because of the grotesqueness of the characterization as well as the apocalyptic nastiness of the plot. It depicts an armada of non-white refugees landing in France which presages the final destruction of Western civilization. At the time, I appreciated immensely its literary quality but was as uncomfortable with the unhappiness of the ending as I had been with Winston Smith's capitulation in the final flaccid denouement of *Nineteen Eighty-four*. It struck me as a work of despair, written by a desperate man devoid of any hope or love. I also felt uneasy at the total lack of true compassion in the novel, indicative perhaps of the war in my own heart between my embittered and entrenched opposition to the presence of non-whites in Britain and a Dickensian love for my fellow man which resisted and transcended the bitter canker of hatred. Looking back at my experience of reading the novel, I am surprised by this retrospective perception of a tension between the intellectual assent of my ideologically addled head to the novel's anti-immigrant message and the rebellion of my healthier and humane heart to the loveless crassness of its plot.

I cannot conclude this exposition of my reading as a seventeen and eighteen-year-old without paying due attention, and paying the debt that's due, to Alexander Solzhenitsyn's magnificent masterpiece, *The Gulag Archipelago*. I have vivid memories of sitting on trains en route to and from the NF's headquarters with my nose in the *Gulag*, devouring volume one and then proceeding directly to the recently published second volume. Even with four hours a day to spend with Solzhenitsyn in the Soviet prison system the reading of these monumental tomes took weeks. They were weeks well-spent, furnishing me with further reasons to oppose communism and reinforcing the uneasiness with Big Government that Orwell had already instilled. There was, however, one major and crucially important difference between the prevailing spirit in Orwell's novel and that in Solzhenitsyn's *Gulag*, and, as I would later discover, in that of Solzhenitsyn's other works also. Whereas Orwell's faithless pessimism permeates his work, Solzhenitsyn's indomitable faith and irrepressible spirit surmounts all the trials and tribulations about which he writes.

The destiny of the small man who dared defy the modern almighty State was epitomized in the eyes of most pessimistic "realists" by the example of Winston Smith in *Nineteen Eighty-Four*. Orwell's novel was published in 1948 while Solzhenitsyn was serving his sentence as a political prisoner of the Soviet regime. As such, the figure of Winston Smith can be seen as not merely a figure of Everyman in his alienation from the centralized State (Big Brother), but as an unwitting figure of Solzhenitsyn himself. According to the "realistic" view, Winston Smith would not only be crushed by the power of the State, he would also betray every ideal, and everything he loved, in abject surrender to the State's Almighty Power. The triumph of Big Brother was inevitable; it was preordained. It was Fate, and to deny or defy fate was fatal and futile.

The fact is, however, that Orwell had failed to shake off the Hegelian determinism of his Marxist past. He had long since become disillusioned with Marxism but still believed that the forces of history were immutable and the triumph of the State inevitable. Orwell still believed, like his former comrades, that proletarian Progress was omnipotent; he differed from them only to the extent that he hated the omnipotent god of Progress, whereas they admired it. Solzhenitsyn, on the other hand, did not believe that such Progress was a god but merely a demon, or a dragon, a manifestation of evil. He did not believe in fate but in freedom; the freedom of the will and its responsibility to serve the truth. Fate was a figment of the imagination, but the dragon was real. Furthermore, it was the duty of the good man to fight the dragon, even unto death if necessary. Solzhenitsyn fought the dragon, even though it was thousands of times bigger than he was, and even though it breathed fire and had killed millions of people. He fought it because, in conscience, he could do nothing else. In doing so, he proved that faith, not fate, is the final victor. Faith can move mountains; it can move tyrannies that were thought to be gods; it can move and remove Big Brother. Solzhenitsyn had re-written George Orwell's novel, replacing the fictional pessimism of Orwell with the triumphant reality of his own life. He represents the victory of Winston Smith. He shows that truth is not only stranger than fiction, it has a happier ending.

I did not know it at the time but Solzhenitsyn's work and the living example of his life would have a transformative influence on my own life. He would sow seeds of faith and hope in my understanding of reality and exorcise the demons of nihilism and pessimism that lurked in the darkest recesses of my soul. Something else I didn't know as I devoured the great Russian's works, and could not have believed in my wildest teenage dreams, was that I would one day meet him at his home in Russia and become his biographer. Twenty years later, in 1998, as I travelled to Russia at his invitation to interview him, I had no idea why he should have granted me an exclusive interview when he had shunned the advances of western writers much more accomplished and better known. He had a reputation as being reclusive and also of being suspicious of journalists and biographers in general, and western journalists and biographers in particular. I was, therefore, mystified by his acceptance of my wishful letter requesting an interview. When I had written it, I had only one published biography to my name. Why on earth would he say "yes" to me when he had said "no" to everyone else? As I pondered this question, it seemed that there was only one likely answer. In my letter I had announced my desire to correct the failure of previous biographies, particularly Michael Scammell's, to pay due attention to Solzhenitsyn's religious beliefs. Perhaps Solzhenitsyn had agreed with my critical assessment and perhaps he shared my desire that a biography be published that emphasized the spiritual dimension of his life and work. Although this seemed the only logical explanation for Solzhenitsyn's surprising acceptance of my request for an interview, it didn't explain why he should think me capable of writing such a book. Perhaps, I thought, Solzhenitsyn knew and admired G. K. Chesterton, the subject of my first, and at that time only, biography, which I had of course mentioned in my letter. Perhaps Solzhenitsyn had thought that anyone who had written a biography of Chesterton was qualified to write sensibly and seriously on religious matters. Perhaps "Chesterton" was the magic word that earned me the interview. This suspicion was confirmed upon my arrival when Solzhenitsyn's wife showed me a dozen or so volumes of the Ignatius Press edition of Chesterton's *Collected Works*. Clearly Solzhenitsyn not only knew Chesterton's works but was an avid collector of them!

Back in 1978, the year in which I had first read Solzhenitsyn, I had not yet read or discovered Chesterton. That discovery remained as an unexpected surprise which would explode on my mind and heart like a beneficent bomb, to borrow Dorothy L. Sayers' evocative description of the impact that Chesterton would have on her own life. In the meantime, the life and work of Alexander Solzhenitsyn would shine forth like a beacon of light amidst the darkness that was enveloping me.

CHAPTER 11

FLIRTING WITH TERRORISM

THE POLITICAL violence in which I had become embroiled since joining the National Front in 1976 would be taken to a whole new level of brutality and danger with my involvement in the Troubles in Northern Ireland. I had been arrested for breaking through police lines and attacking pro-IRA demonstrators on a Troops Out Movement march at Hyde Park in London and was eager in my militant zeal to become more involved in what I considered the war being fought in Ulster (the six counties in the north of Ireland) between the Protestant Loyalists and the Catholic Republicans.

Put at its simplest, the Troubles in Northern Ireland, which had erupted into communal violence in 1969, were a conflict between the Protestant majority and the Catholic minority. The Protestants called themselves Loyalists because of their loyalty to the United Kingdom. The Catholics called themselves Nationalists or Republicans because of their desire that the six counties in the north be united with the twenty-six counties of the Irish Republic in the south. By the end of the 1970s more than two thousand people had been killed in the political struggle in Ulster and the figure would rise to more than thirty-five-hundred before the Good Friday Agreement in 1998 brought a faltering peace to the Province.

My fanatical support for the Loyalist cause, which had already manifested itself in my learning of the best-known Loyalist songs, such as "The Sash My Father Wore," "No Surrender," and "The Old Orange Flute," was as intemperate as my fanatical support for the National Front. I was impatient to become more actively involved in the Troubles and in October 1978 I jumped at the opportunity to travel to Londonderry at the invitation of a new branch of the Young National Front, which had been formed in the Protestant Waterside district of that most troubled and divided of cities. Londonderry, as it is called by the Protestants, or Derry as the Catholics prefer to call it, was one of the flashpoints of the Troubles. Unlike Northern Ireland as a whole, Londonderry had a Catholic majority. As such, the Protestants, most of whom lived in the Waterside to the south-east of the River Foyle, felt under siege. The Catholics who lived on the other side of the river were amongst the most militant supporters of the IRA in the whole of Northern Ireland. The Catholic Bogside, just across the river from the Waterside, had been the scene of bloody riots in 1969 which many consider to be the definitive beginning of the Troubles. The Bogside had also been the scene of the infamous Bloody Sunday in January 1972 when fourteen Catholic rioters were shot dead by the British Army. I was aware, therefore, that I was arriving into a cauldron of hatred and sectarian violence. I had no idea, however, that I was arriving on the eve of a storm, the violence of which would make the previous year's Battle of Lewisham seem a mere skirmish by comparison.

The scenario as I arrived was one of brooding anticipation of the hell that everyone expected was about to break loose. Sinn Fein, the political wing of the IRA, had organized a march, the route of which would cross the bridge over the River Foyle into the Protestant Waterside. Reacting to this provocation, Ian Paisley, leader of the Democratic Unionist Party, had organized a Loyalist march from the Waterside, the planned route of which would cross the bridge at the same time as the Republican march, thereby causing a confrontation between the two sides on the bridge itself. Faced with this stand-off between violent and irreconcilable foes, the Royal Ulster Constabulary found itself in an impossible position. Clearly they could not allow both marches to go ahead with the inevitable deaths and bloodshed that would have been the result. Realizing that they had a riot on their hands, whichever decision was made, the RUC chose the easier option, which was the lesser of the two riots. Knowing the militancy of the Catholics of the Bogside and mindful of the deaths on Bloody Sunday and the history of other riots in the Catholic area of the city, the RUC chose to ban the Loyalist march in the hope that the ensuing anger of the Protestant community in the Waterside could be more easily and less violently contained.

On the morning of the IRA march, the small group of local YNF members held an impromptu march of our own behind an improvised National Front banner. As we made our way down to where the Loyalists would be gathering we were applauded loudly by those who saw us. The news had made its way through the grapevine that an Englishman from the controversial National Front had flown all the way from London to offer his support, turning me into something of a celebrity. As we turned a corner I was confronted with a sight, the likes of which I had never seen before. Rows upon rows of armored cars blocked the streets in front of us, preventing the gathering Loyalists from getting anywhere near the bridge over which their hated enemy would soon be marching. Everything remained relatively calm until the Loyalist mob caught sight of the Republican marchers crossing the bridge amidst a forest of Irish tricolours. As if on cue, the Loyalists began attacking the lines of armed police with bricks, stones, and petrol bombs. Running battles ensued which lasted for hours, until well after dark, during which shops were looted and burned to the ground and dozens of people, including almost seventy police officers were injured.

At some stage during these hours of anarchy I found myself in a Loyalist mob that had decided to attack Gobnascale, the only Catholic enclave on the Protestant side of the river. Rumors spread that the police would turn a blind eye to such an attack, though in retrospect I find it difficult to believe that the police would have been in any mood to cooperate with a rioting mob that had spent the day attacking them with such irrepressible violence. In any event, there were few if any police present when we arrived at the road that led down to the Catholic community. A crowd of young Republicans was waiting for us, no doubt expecting our arrival and intent on defending their homes and community from attack. I found myself in the vanguard of the charge as we descended on our opponents, hurling a hail of rocks at them as we went. After throwing their own volley of rocks at us, the Republican mob turned on its heels and fled. Sensing victory, I charged forward intent on taking the fight into the very streets of Gobnascale. I discovered, however, that I was the only person still charging forward. Not wishing to commit suicide, I went back towards the Loyalist mob which was now looking at me as though I was mad. I berated them for their cowardice, but I realize now that they were streetwise whereas I was stupid, indeed almost fatally so. I came to understand later what the Loyalist mob had understood then, namely that the street on which we were charging would have been guarded by IRA snipers, ready to shoot if any of the Loyalist assailants had strayed too close. It would not be the last time that I would be preserved from possibly fatal stupidity by luck or providence, saved by the skin of my teeth by the grace of God.

Inflamed with new enthusiasm by my experience in Londonderry, I joined the Orange Order, an anti-Catholic secret society committed to the Loyalist cause, and learned its rituals, its secret handshake, and its annual passwords. Prior to attending the regular lodge meetings in Hounslow, Middlesex, on the western edge of London, I would meet up for a few pints with a fellow NF member and Orangeman. Neither of us was a believing Protestant, he an atheist and I an agnostic, but we were united by our Loyalism and anti-Catholicism. Proceeding to the meeting after several pints of ale, he and I would share a surreptitious smirk of contempt as the lodge chaplain read from Scripture.

My Loyalist sympathies got me in trouble with members of London's Irish community. On one occasion, in a cellar bar in Soho in the seedier part of the West End, I was knocked unconscious when struck on the head from behind with a chair by someone who objected to my singing of Orange songs. I never saw my assailant coming and the experience brought home to me the wisdom of my father's words that it was always wise in a pub to sit with one's back to the wall. On another occasion, I had my nose broken by an Irishman in the Amersham Arms in New Cross. I was alone and somehow managed to get into an altercation with a group of Irishmen about politics. I came off second best and am thankful that my assailant's jab was so straight. If instead of a straight jab he had hit me with a hook, I could have been living with a crooked nose for the rest of my life! Thank God for small mercies! I still possess the book that I was carrying when this fight happened. It sits on my shelf downstairs as a blood spattered reminder of a long lost battle.

As a loyal Orangeman, the highlight of the year was the annual Twelfth of July parade when the Orange Order celebrates the victory of the Protestant William of Orange against the Catholic King James II at the Battle of the Boyne in 1690. Although I had attended the English Twelfth in Southport, just north of Liverpool, the experience was utterly eclipsed by my attendance at the mother of all Twelfth of July parades, held annually in Belfast, at which tens of thousands of Orangemen, accompanied by hundreds of flute and accordion bands, are cheered on by tens of thousands more who line the streets waving Union flags as the parade of Orange lodges passes by. There's nothing like it and the memory still sends a primal, tribal thrill up my spine as I remember the beating of the drums and the sheer fervor and magnitude of the event.

On the eve of the parade it is customary for the Protestant communities in Northern Ireland to build huge bonfires, which become the focus for street parties well into the night. I spent the night of the Eleventh on the Shankill Road, a staunchly militant Protestant enclave in west Belfast surrounded by hostile Catholic communities. As the night progressed and the intake of alcohol increased I found myself at a lively party in a house full of friendly strangers. All was going well if somewhat hazily until a group of men knocked on the door demanding to know if the person they were looking for was in the house. The men were from the Ulster Defence Association (or UDA), armed gunmen, who, fuelled by alcohol, were looking to settle an old score with the man in question. This was my introduction to the seedier side of Loyalism in which paramilitaries emerge not as freedom fighters but as gangsters and drunken thugs. My hosts told the gunmen that the person they sought was not in the house. The gunmen were not convinced and said so. They left but warned that they would be back. I then discovered that the wanted man was indeed in the house and the whole party was thrown into a state of fear and confusion. In my inebriated state and not thinking of the consequences, I volunteered to leave the house in search of police protection for the family. It was seen as an act of great heroism, or perhaps quixotic foolishness, but my offer was accepted in an instant. Whether I was numbed by alcohol or by sheer ignorance of the danger I was in, I left the house half expecting to be met by the gunmen but not feeling particularly scared. Perhaps I believed that I would be protected by my English accent and the fact that I was a stranger and therefore aloof from the internecine disputes of the neighborhood. In the event, the path was clear. I made my way to the Crumlin Road where I flagged down an armored police car, the same sort I had seen for the first time in Londonderry. I explained the situation to the police and they told me to jump in the back of the vehicle. It was only then, surrounded by heavily-armed and clearly nervous police officers, that the reality of the danger I had been in finally dawned on me.

On the following morning, still slightly drunk, I followed the parade, reveling in the sheer fervor and flavor of the music, the flags and the cheering crowds. As the parade reached Sandy Row, another staunchly and militantly Protestant area, I decided to stop and watch the remainder of the parade pass by. Afterwards I retreated to a local pub to immerse myself in the celebratory atmosphere. Some time and several pints later I decided to wend my way back to the Shankill Road and asked the people with whom I had been imbibing which was the shortest way. I was informed, in no uncertain terms, that the shortest way was not an option as it passed through a Catholic area. Becoming insanely belligerent under the influence of alcohol, I insisted that I would not be intimidated by supporters of the IRA and intended to take the shortest route to my destination. If I had followed my own drunken inclination, I would have been dead within the hour. I have no real doubt about that.

It would have been extremely unlikely that a drunk and brawny stranger could have walked through the militant Catholic neighborhood, on the edge of the notorious Falls Road, without being stopped and questioned, especially on the Twelfth of July of all days when the IRA would have been more vigilant than ever in protecting its own communities. Having been stopped and questioned, my English accent and close-cropped hair would have marked me as a British soldier, itself a guaranteed death sentence in such a neighborhood. Any attempt on my part to tell them that I was not a soldier but someone who had come to Northern Ireland to celebrate the Twelfth of July would hardly have proved less fatal.

I recall people trying to restrain me as I sought to leave the pub and a young couple, older than me but probably still in their twenties, suggested that I come home with them for something to eat. This seemed a convivial option and I accepted their invitation. We drove to their home in an affluent area of south Belfast, where they gave me some food and endeavored to sober me up with a pot of tea. I am now aware that this kind couple probably saved my life and it saddens me that I have no way of thanking them. Their names never emerged from the boozy fog into which my mind had wandered.

The vigilance of the Catholic communities in Belfast was brought home to me on a subsequent visit when our two NF minibuses came under attack with rocks thrown from youths in the Unity Flats complex which bordered the Shankill Road. As we drove from the Shankill Road towards Belfast city center we were met with a hail of rocks and bricks. The drivers panicked and took a sharp right turn, only to discover that this led us round the block, forcing us to pass the waiting Republican youths for a second time. Clearly our arrival on the Shankill Road in minibuses with mainland number plates had been monitored. Forewarned and forearmed, the Republican youths waited in ambush for our return journey. Nobody was hurt and only minor damage was done to our vehicles but it served as a timely reminder that we were in the midst of a city in the grip of a civil war.

I was a regular visitor to Ulster between 1978 and 1985 and became associated with the leadership of the Ulster Defence Association (UDA) and the Ulster Volunteer Force (UVF), the two main Loyalist paramilitary organizations. I visited the UDA headquarters for meetings with the UDA's commander, Andy Tyrie, and Deputy Commander, John McMichael. As an impressionable young man, I naïvely hero-worshipped Tyrie who had been immortalized in the Loyalist song "We'll Fight in the Bogside" as "our bold leader Andy who stands to the fore." When I met him for the first time, I felt as though I was in the presence of a living legend, the leader of a fearless organization which was taking the fight to the enemy by assassinating IRA members.

Tyrie treated me very warmly, as a friend and ally, though whether this was connected to a sense of flattery I have no idea. John McMichael was always very friendly and polite, though I sensed that it was more from a respectful deference to his commander's warmth towards me than to any genuine sense of friendship or political affinity. McMichael's benign and gentle appearance belied the fact that he was Commander of the feared Ulster Freedom Fighters (UFF), the UDA's military wing which was known to have carried out many political assassinations and bombings. In spite of his involvement in the planning of terrorist activities, McMichael was seen by some, myself included, as a moderate and compromising voice in Ulster's convoluted politics, favoring dialogue with the enemy. I saw all such talk of compromise as tantamount to surrender and supported the strategy of total war. McMichael was murdered by the IRA in December 1987 when a bomb planted under his car was detonated as he left to deliver Christmas turkeys to Loyalist prisoners. It is widely believed that the IRA received crucial intelligence information from McMichael's enemies within the UDA itself, enabling the IRA to target him successfully. A little over two months later, Andy Tyrie narrowly escaped death when he was also the victim of a car bomb. Tyrie was convinced that the device was planted by his enemies within the UDA and announced his retirement from the organization.

I was not on such intimate terms with the leadership of the UVF but I had two meetings with members of this organization, considered by many to be even more violent and extreme than the UDA, both of which have left an indelible mark on my memory. On the first occasion I was summoned to a UVF social club on the Shankill Road, one of the many such clubs owned by paramilitary groups on both sides of the religious divide. I was not told the reason for my being summoned but arrived dutifully at the appointed hour. I was ushered through a labyrinth of corridors, seeming to backtrack on circuitous routes on several occasions, which had the effect of disorientation, presumably intentional. Finally I was led into a windowless room at which four men, evidently senior members of the UVF's high command, sat behind a desk facing me. I was asked to take a seat and a friendly, though formal conversation took place. They told me of intelligence information they had received about the recent Toxteth riots in Liverpool, which would date the meeting to the latter half of 1981. (The black community in Toxteth had rioted against the police in July 1981, no doubt in emulation of the Brixton riots earlier in the year at which I had been present.) I feigned interest in the information they offered but suspected that this was merely their polite way of breaking the ice by showing that they were sympathetic with the NF's struggle against the blacks on the mainland.

It was, as I suspected, the prelude to a discussion of the crux of the matter for which I had been summoned. They spoke with interest about the connections they imagined I had with neo-Nazi organizations in Europe and the United States and wondered whether these connections might be used by the UVF as a means of smuggling guns to Northern Ireland. They had also heard that senior members of the NF had connections with Arab countries, including Colonel Gaddafi's Libya, and wondered if these might prove fruitful avenues for the smuggling of guns from the Arab world to Ulster. Wishing to sound responsive and helpful, I assured them that I would do what I could to make connections with neo-Nazi groups on the UVF's behalf and that I did indeed know people who had connections with the Arab world. In truth, I had no desire to become involved, even remotely, with the dirty and dangerous business of gun-running but it would not have been prudent and might have been foolhardy to have been so candid at the time. My own connections with European and American neo-Nazis were not very extensive and I did not consider myself part of the militantly pro-Arab faction in the NF, the members of which were forging links with Gaddafi and others in the Middle East. The nearest I came to involvement with the Arabs was the receipt of an invitation to attend a reception at the Saudi Arabian Embassy in London. I would have attended, out of pure curiosity if for no other reason, but the invitation arrived whilst I was in prison.

In spite of my own unwillingness to become too directly involved in the terrorist operations in Northern Ireland, I was very much aware, as were the leaders of the UVF and UDA, that National Front members serving with the army in Northern Ireland were smuggling intelligence information on IRA suspects to the Loyalist paramilitaries. This information included photographs of the suspected IRA men, their home addresses, the type of car they drove and its registration number, and other useful facts. I have little doubt that such information was used by the UVF and UDA to target and assassinate their enemies.

My second close encounter with the Ulster Volunteer Force happened outside another UVF social club, this time in Rathcoole, a Protestant housing estate in Newtownabbey, north of Belfast. I was in the club with some Young National Front colleagues, enjoying the Loyalist songs being sung by the group on stage, when I received a pat on the shoulder.

Looking up, I was told that I was wanted outside. The news alarmed me somewhat. Who wanted to see me outside and why? I racked my brain for anything I might have done or said which might have offended a local paramilitary godfather. Feeling nervous, I followed the person outside to find three young men, about my age or perhaps a year or two older, waiting for me. The leader of the group did all the talking and informed me that they were an active service unit of the UVF who had become disillusioned with the UVF's leadership. They desired to put themselves under my sole command, promising to "take out" (i.e. kill) any targets that I wanted eliminated. The initial relief at not being "taken out" myself evaporated in the presence of this unusual and frightening offer. For all my extremism, I had no desire to kill anybody, or to have someone kill anybody for me. Sensing my hesitation and wondering whether I doubted their earnestness, the leader offered to show me their arsenal of weapons. I declined politely, assuring him that I believed him, and promised that I would be in touch about his proposal, never at any stage intending to keep the promise. I heard a year or so later that the leader of the group had been arrested for shooting dead the mother of an IRA man on her own doorstep. I shudder to think that such blood could easily have been on my hands.

Another of my contacts in Northern Ireland was George Seawright, an outspoken and fiery Unionist politician and a secret member of the UVF. I had interviewed him for *Nationalism Today*, in which he declared his support for the NF's policy on race and immigration, as well as for its Loyalist policy on Northern Ireland. Seawright was a firebrand, even by Ulster standards, and in 1984 received a six month suspended prison sentence for an inflammatory speech in which he apparently suggested that Catholics should be burned. In the midst of a heated public debate, he proclaimed that any Northern Irish Catholics who objected to the singing of the British national anthem were "just Fenian scum who have been indoctrinated by the Catholic Church." Taxpayers' money should be spent, he proclaimed, on an incinerator, in which such "scum" should be thrown, "burning the lot of them." Adding insult to injury, he added that "their priests should be thrown in and burnt as well."*

In November of the following year, Seawright was amongst a group of Loyalist protestors who physically attacked Tom King, the British Government's Secretary of State for Northern Ireland, for his part in the Anglo-Irish Agreement. Eleven months later, in October 1986, Seawright was sentenced to nine months in prison for his part in the attack. On November 19, 1987, he was shot on the Shankill Road by members of the Irish People's Liberation Organisation, dying of his wounds two weeks later, only a few days before the IRA bomb killed John McMichael.

My connections with revolutionary groups outside of the National Front was not limited to the Protestant Loyalists. Although I did not have extensive connections with neo-Nazi groups in Europe, there was one notable exception, though the group in question would be more accurately described as neo-fascist than neo-Nazi. The group

---

* *Belfast Telegraph*, May 31, 1984

was Terza Posizione (Third Position), an Italian neo-fascist organization, the leaders of which had been accused of involvement in the horrific bombing of Bologna railway station in August 1980, in which eighty-five people were killed and more than two hundred injured. In the wake of the bombing the Italian government issued twenty-eight arrest warrants against leading neo-fascists who were believed to have had some measure of involvement in the bombing. Several of the leaders of Terza Posizione were amongst those for whom arrest warrants were issued. Escaping from Italy to avoid arrest, they made their way to England and were hidden in safe houses by NF members and sympathizers in the coastal town of Brighton, fifty miles south of London.

Over the next few years, during his period of exile in England, I got to know Roberto Fiore, the leader of Terza Posizione, very well. He and his comrades added a certain sophistication to the Nationalist scene in England, or so it seemed at the time. Whereas the NF's membership was becoming more proletarian, comprised largely of young and disaffected skinheads, our Italian confreres were clearly better educated and more cultured. I remember Roberto playing Beethoven's *Für Elise* on the piano, not the most challenging piece perhaps but still beyond my ability or that of any of my English friends. He and his comrades led quasi-military training exercises for members of the Young National Front on a secluded estate in Hampshire and we were all duly impressed by their mastery of the martial arts. They saw themselves not merely as ideological radicals but as political soldiers, an image which became all the rage amongst the younger and more radical elements of the NF.

Although the alleged involvement of Fiore and Terza Posizione in the Bologna bombing was widely known, it was never mentioned. My experience in Northern Ireland had taught me the importance of always acting on a "need to know" basis, which meant never asking any questions if you did not need to know the answer. Curiosity was dangerous. If one knew nothing incriminating, one could not be incriminated oneself, nor could one incriminate others. I suspected then and am convinced now that Fiore and his comrades were not responsible for the bombing, but were simply the victims of a state-sponsored witch-hunt. In the wake of the bombing and the understandable anger which accompanied it, there was a need for scapegoats, at least until the real perpetrators were caught.

I liked Roberto Fiore very much and found him pleasant, intelligent, and affable company. One of the last times I ever saw him was in 1985 when he and I travelled together from London to Cheshire for Nick Griffin's wedding. By this time I was becoming interested in Catholicism and I recall a lengthy conversation with Fiore in which he seemed to share my own Catholic sympathies but confessed that he was not a believer. He thought that Catholicism was a necessary part of a healthy European culture but he did not believe in the Divinity of Christ. I believe that he is now a practicing Catholic.

Like Nick Griffin, Roberto Fiore has prospered politically in the years since I knew him. In 1997, following the declaration of an amnesty by the Italian government, he returned to Italy and founded Forza Nuova (New Force), an Italian political party of which he is now the leader, which advocates the banning of abortion and the encouragement of the traditional family. Like Nick Griffin, he is a Member of the European Parliament.

I have also prospered, though in a very different way, since the years in which I flirted with terrorism. Others were not so fortunate. I recall once more John McMichael and George Seawright, one killed by an IRA bomb and the other by a terrorist bullet. If it were not for luck and the grace of God my own ending might have been as ugly and as brutal. I have much for which to be grateful.

CHAPTER 12

HATRED AND HOOLIGANISM

Blue is the colour,
Football is the game,
We're all together
And winning is our aim.

—Official song of Chelsea Football Club

I HAVE abandoned many things on my journey from racial hatred to rational love but one passion that has stayed with me, unchanging through all the years, is my allegiance to Chelsea Football Club. Today, Chelsea is one of the biggest clubs in the world, ranked alongside Barcelona, Real Madrid, AC Milan, Inter Milan, Juventus, Bayern Munich, and Manchester United in the elite of world soccer. It was not always so. As I grew up Chelsea was in decline and would remain in the doldrums throughout most of the 1970s and 1980s. During this period I attended games regularly and played a not insignificant part in the increase of hooliganism amongst Chelsea's "blue and white army" of supporters.

My association with Chelsea Football Club began innocently enough. In the years of my childhood, in the late sixties, Chelsea had an entertaining young team which never really fulfilled its potential. There were many Chelsea supporters amongst my childhood friends and we fantasized about being our favorite players as we played soccer on the field opposite my house in Haverhill, adjacent to the local Catholic church. My favorite player was the Chelsea goalkeeper, Peter Bonetti, and I was thrilled one Christmas to receive a Chelsea goalkeeper's shirt and a pair of Peter Bonetti trademark gloves. I remember watching the FA Cup Final in 1970 and being on the edge of my seat as Chelsea came from behind to lift the trophy for the first time in its history. I also remember my parents being confused and perhaps even a little alarmed at the extremes of emotion that I exhibited as I watched the game.

After we moved to London in 1973, I was finally able to travel to Stamford Bridge, Chelsea's stadium, to watch my beloved team in the flesh. The team was now in definite decline and would be relegated to the lower division a couple of years later. As the team lost with depressing frequency, its supporters reacted with increasing violence. By the mid-seventies Chelsea's supporters had perhaps the worst reputation for hooliganism of all the rival groups of supporters in the country, and this at a time when violence at soccer games was at its height. As a fourteen- or fifteen-year-old, I was too young to be among the leaders of Chelsea's marauding army of supporters but I was happy to run with the pack. Away games were the most thrilling as several thousand Chelsea supporters descended on opponents' stadiums and towns like a swarm of locusts, or a Viking horde. There were running battles between rival supporters, with bricks being thrown through shop windows and supporters brawling in the streets. At an away game in Bristol my own attempts at rowdiness were stopped by a police officer who punched me in the solar plexus, taking the wind from my body literally and from my sails figuratively. It became customary for business owners to board up their shops and for pubs to lock their doors in anticipation of the arrival of the blue and white army. There was something sordidly thrilling about instilling such fear into a community and I'm ashamed at the ignoble pleasure that it gave me.

Another unpleasant feature amongst soccer fans at the time, and amongst Chelsea fans more than most, was a rampant and aggressive racism. There were relatively few black players in those days but they were routinely greeted with abusive chants and monkey noises whenever they touched the ball. This endemic racism would prove fertile ground for the National Front and I would make a point of targeting football supporters when writing for *Bulldog*.

In 1978, when Tottenham Hotspur signed two Argentinian players, Osvaldo Ardiles and Ricardo Villa, the Anti-Nazi League handed out flyers at games stating that the National Front opposed the signing of the players because they were immigrants. I responded by publishing a leaflet stating that the two players were welcomed by the NF because they were white and that it was the Anti-Nazi League who opposed these players because they came from a fascist country, Argentina being ruled by a military junta at the time. The flyers were a huge success and confirmed in my mind the strategy of making football supporters a target for NF propaganda. The back page of *Bulldog* was dedicated to encouraging racist behavior amongst soccer fans. I launched the Racist League which encouraged football hooligans to report racist activity amongst their own club's supporters in the hope of being awarded points for "good" racist behavior.

In terms of sales, the strategy of selling *Bulldog* at football stadiums was a huge success. At Chelsea in the late 1970s we were selling seven hundred copies of *Bulldog* to crowds of as small as nine thousand. The low attendance was the consequence of the team's faltering fortunes, whereas the high sales of *Bulldog* were the result of the rise of racism and hooliganism, which seemed to go hand-in-glove. The Chelsea Headhunters, one of the most feared gangs of football hooligans, were associated not only with the racism of the National Front but also with the Loyalism of Northern Ireland. The Headhunters forged links with supporters of Glasgow Rangers, a Scottish team known for its anti-Catholic sectarianism and the militant Orangism and Loyalism of its supporters. Rangers fans held their arms up in what looked like a fascist salute to signify the Red Hand of Ulster, the symbol of Loyalism. When Chelsea fans adopted this salute they did so with the dual meaning deliberately in mind. It was meant to symbolize their Ulster Loyalism and hatred of the IRA but was also a brazen Nazi salute to signify their unapologetic racism. It was not uncommon at Chelsea away games to see hundreds of hands outstretched in this fashion, resembling a Nuremberg rally in the era of the Third Reich.

Another ruthless and violent gang of football hooligans was the Inter-City Firm, or ICF, a mob of thugs who followed West Ham United. Sales of *Bulldog* were almost as high at West Ham's stadium as they were at Chelsea's. Every weekend *Bulldog* was sold at soccer stadiums up and down the country, registering large sales and contributing to the culture of hatred which seemed to be spreading with alarming speed. I have little doubt that this success at soccer grounds was one of the reasons that the Director of Public Prosecutions decided to charge me with offences under the Race Relations Act.

I had long since ceased to run with the pack at Chelsea, preferring to direct operations from a distance as editor of *Bulldog*, but I still liked to attend games on the odd and increasingly rare Saturdays when the National Front did not have a demonstration at which my attendance was expected. On one occasion I was ejected from the stadium by a police officer who recognized my face from his policing of NF activities, but for the most part I managed to disappear within the comforting anonymity of the crowd. I would like, however, to conclude this brief detour into the violent world of football hooliganism with an episode which has resonated with me across the years as a powerful act of charity.

It was early November 1978, only a few short weeks after my return from the riots in Londonderry, and I decided to go to watch Chelsea play in a game against local West London rivals, Queens Park Rangers. The game was at QPR's stadium in Shepherd's Bush and I arrived early to ensure that I could secure a ticket. As it was still several hours before kick-off, I retired to a local pub to kill time. I walked to the stadium shortly before the game was due to start and took my place amongst the Chelsea fans. Almost immediately I was ejected from the stadium by a police officer. Undeterred, I spent the last of my money on another ticket and once again entered the stadium. The same policeman, astonished at my perseverance, ejected me for a second time. I had no money to buy another ticket but was determined to see the game. In desperation, I approached a police officer on duty outside the stadium and made up a pathetic story of how I'd been mugged and had all my money stolen. With a chutzpah and brazenness fueled by the quantity of ale I'd consumed, I asked the policeman if I could borrow the money for a ticket to the ground, promising to pay him back if he gave me his address. I could see that he did not believe me and he must have smelled the alcohol on my breath. Nonetheless, he lent me the money and gave me the address of the local police station as the place to which the money should be sent to repay the debt. He must have expected never to see the money again, especially as I had not offered to give my own address. I was deeply moved by this act of charity and genuine human kindness, this practical example of loving one's neighbor, and it has stayed with me all these years. I sent him the money, of course, and hope that my act of gratitude reinforced his trust in his fellow man. As I ponder the power of this singular and seemingly unimportant episode, it continues to shine forth the love of neighbor and the happiness it brings. How different was the heart of this one good man from my own cankered heart, filled with the hatred of my neighbor and the misery it causes.

CHAPTER 13

SKINHEADS AND SKREWDRIVER

ALONGSIDE MY love for soccer, pop music was the other great passion of my childhood and youth. I used to march around the school playing field with a group of friends, around 1968 when I was seven-years-old, singing "Yellow Submarine" and "She Loves You" by the Beatles. John, Paul, George, and Ringo were part of the very fabric of the sixties, their presence being felt even by those who were too young to know what was going on. Oddly enough, however, it was Elvis and not the Beatles who captured my imagination as a child. I remember the father of a friend playing some of his records and being thrilled by the sheer exuberance of "Teddy Bear," "I Need Your Love Tonight," and "A Fool Such As I." Elvis had a certain *je ne sais quoi* which put him in a class of his own. Years later, during my descent into bigotry, Elvis' gospel music would be my only connection to the hope-filled message of Christianity, a thin thread of light in the gathering gloom.

At the age of eleven I began to spend most of my pocket money on records, buying a new hit single every week. Glam rock was all the rage and David Bowie became one of my idols. Bowie would get himself into trouble in the seventies for his own brief flirtation with fascism. In an interview in 1974 he betrayed an admiration for Hitler, describing the Führer as "one of the first rock stars:" "Look at some of the films and see how he moved. I think he was quite as good as Jagger. . . . [Hitler] used politics and theatrics and created this thing that governed and controlled the show for those twelve years. The world will never see his like again. He staged a country."* In the following year, rather bizarrely considering his own androgynous image, he ranted against decadence and called for an extreme right-wing solution to the problem: "I think that morals should be straightened up for a start. They're disgusting. There will be a political figure in the not too distant future who'll sweep through this part of the world like early rock 'n' roll did. You probably hope I'm not right but I am. . . . You've got to have an extreme right front come up and sweep everything off its feet and tidy everything up. Then you can get a new form of liberalism." It is easy to imagine that the choice of the phrase "extreme right front" would have been seen as a veiled reference to the National Front, which was definitely in the ascendant at the time.

In April 1976 Bowie was detained by customs officials on the Russian/Polish border after they discovered a cache of Nazi memorabilia in his luggage. In the same

---

* All quotes about Bowie's flirtation with fascism are taken from David Buckley, *Strange Fascination: David Bowie—The Definitive Story*, London: Virgin Books, 2001, pp. 289-95

month, after a concert in the Swedish capital, Stockholm, Bowie was more forthright than ever in his candid expression of fascist sympathies: "I believe Britain could benefit from a Fascist leader. After all, Fascism is really nationalism." Six days after the pro-fascist remarks in Sweden, Bowie returned to England and allegedly gave a Nazi salute from the back of an open-top limo to the crowd of fans assembled at Victoria station to greet him. It is also widely believed that Bowie visited Hitler's bunker in Berlin and had photographer Andy Kent photograph him with his arm outstretched in a Nazi salute. Kent was made to swear that he would never release the photograph to the press, a promise that the photographer has dutifully kept.

Given my admiration for Bowie's music, it is hardly surprising that I rejoiced in the news that he had given a Nazi salute to his fans. I wrote in *Bulldog* a few years later that Bowie was "the Big Daddy of Futurism" who, on his early album *Hunky Dory*, "started the anti-Communist musical tradition which we now see flourishing amidst the new wave of Futurist bands." It is customary for music journalists to dismiss Bowie's dallying with fascism as a brief flirtation caused by drug-induced manic depression, in other words by a temporary madness, but it is curious, as I mentioned in the *Bulldog* article, that the much earlier *Hunky Dory* album, recorded in 1971, contains several tracks that are suggestive of Nietzschean philosophy and Nazi sympathy. In "Quicksand" Bowie places himself into the mind of Hitler in the bunker as the Third Reich crumbles around him, contemplating suicide and condemning Churchill's lies, and remaining defiantly unrepentant to the last. "Song for

Bob Dylan," for all its ambiguity and ambivalence, seems to climax with apparent disdain for Robert Zimmerman as "every nation's refugee," blaming Dylan's leftist radicalism and iconoclasm for breaking up the unity of the family. Such a reading of the lyrics dovetails with Bowie's later pro-fascist comments. In addition, Bowie's stripping away of Dylan's adopted stage name, his mask, to address him by his real name of Zimmerman could be seen, arguably at least, as veiled anti-Semitism, removing the gentile mask to expose the Jew behind it. "Andy Warhol" seems to mock the pretentiousness of its subject, which would explain why Warhol disapproved of it. "Oh! You Pretty Things" is a Nietzschean anthem exhibiting contempt for homo sapiens who "have outgrown their use" and who need to "make way for the Homo Superior." Homo sapiens are the *untermenschen* who are superseded by the emergence of homo superior, the übermensch or Superman from which the Nazis derived their notions of the Master Race. Since the quazi-Nazi Nietzscheanism of the *Hunky Dory* album came five years before Bowie's fascist declarations in 1976 and the Nazi kitsch of *Heroes* came a year after, it is a trifle naïve and simplistic to dismiss Bowie's fascist flirtation as a mere fling or one-night-stand. It would be more accurate to see it as a tempestuous and sordid love affair lasting several years.

In any event, I was clutching at straws or straw men in trying to claim Bowie as a true fellow traveler with me and my comrades in the National Front. He was as nebulous as the clouds and as changeable as the weather. What I wanted, and what the Young National Front needed, were new bands that would embrace our creed and have the courage to proclaim it in their music. The need was great in the late-seventies because of the advent of punk rock, which had politicized rock music in the direction of anarchy, socialism and nihilism.

In August 1976, in the wake of Bowie's widely publicized comments, a group of left-wing activities founded Rock Against Racism, destined to be a powerful force in the fight against racism amongst young people and, in consequence, a major enemy in my own battle to incite racial hatred. The sparks that ignited Rock Against Racism were not the words of David Bowie but those of Eric Clapton during a concert in Birmingham. Obviously under the influence of drugs or alcohol, or both, Clapton told the audience that he supported the anti-immigration policies of the controversial former Conservative MP, Enoch Powell. He told the crowd that England had "become overcrowded" and that they should vote for Powell to stop Britain from becoming "a black colony." Becoming more abusive, he shouted that Britain should "get the foreigners out, get the wogs out, get the coons out," and then proceeded to chant the NF slogan "Keep Britain White."

Rock Against Racism was a huge success. In early 1978, an estimated 100,000 people marched the six miles from Trafalgar Square to Victoria Park in London's East End in an event organized jointly by Rock Against Racism and the Anti-Nazi League. Many of the biggest punk bands played in the free festival which followed the march, including the Clash, Buzzcocks, Steel Pulse, X-Ray Spex, the Ruts, Generation X, the Tom Robinson Band, and Sham 69. In an act of defiant opposition, I was amongst a group of

Young National Front activists who heckled the march as it wended its way past the Bladebone pub, a well-known NF meeting place in Bethnal Green. By this time the skinhead movement was growing and we had many skinheads in our ranks, barracking the punks and other "degenerates" as they walked past. Occasionally we would see groups of skinheads amongst the marchers and would challenge them to leave the march and join us, insisting that no true skinhead could support the Anti-Nazi League. A surprising number heeded our call, leaving the ranks of the anti-racist marchers and joining the ranks of the racists instead. This indicated that many of those on the march had joined it for the music and not the politics. Nonetheless, the huge size of this anti-racist demonstration illustrated the power of rock music to lure tens of thousands of youngsters to active participation in the political struggle.

The lesson that I learned from this event was that rock music was a powerful weapon and that the Young National Front had to learn how to wield it as successfully as our enemies. I started Rock Against Communism to try to counter the impact of Rock Against Racism and, from this time on, rock music was a major feature of every issue of *Bulldog*.

From its very inception, Rock Against Communism was largely a skinhead phenomenon. The skinhead scene had exploded in the wake of the punk movement and was largely a reaction against it. As punk became more radical, aligning itself with political causes such as Rock Against Racism or the Anti-Nazi League, racist punks simply shaved their heads in protest. The first two bands to enjoy a large skinhead following were Sham 69 and Skrewdriver, both of which had their first records released in 1977. Sham 69 alienated large sections of their own audience when they decided to support Rock Against Racism. At a concert at London's Rainbow Theatre in September 1979, groups of skinheads who supported either the National Front or the more extreme and openly neo-Nazi British Movement chanted "there's only one Adolf Hitler" before the band came on stage, setting the scene for what would follow. As Sham 69 began to play, the skinheads greeted them with a barrage of Nazi salutes and repeated chants of *Sieg Heil!* ("Hail, victory!"). Invading the stage, the skinheads continued their Nazi chants and salutes as fighting broke out amongst rival factions in the audience, beer cans and bottles being hurled, forcing the band to abandon the show. Similar scenes erupted at other of the bands concerts, including one particularly violent concert at Middlesex Polytechnic which was abandoned after NF and BM skinheads rushed the stage. With their own audience turning against them in protest at their support for Rock Against Racism, Sham 69 were forced to cease playing live concerts.

Skrewdriver, the other major skinhead band at the time, were former punks who had shaved their hair because, in the words of lead singer Ian Stuart, "punk music at the time was becoming too left-wing."* I had bought the band's debut album, *All Skrewed Up*, which was released in late 1977, but would not meet Ian Stuart until 1979, by which

---

* Joe Pearce, *Skrewdriver: The First Ten Years*, London: Skrewdriver Services, 1987, p. 6

time he had become a member of the Young National Front. We met in the Hoop and Grapes pub on Farringdon Street in central London, an odd choice of location considering that it was near the office of the *Morning Star*, the Communist Party's newspaper, and was popular with the paper's journalists and print workers. Ian had returned to London to try to reform Skrewdriver who had split up the previous year. He was friends with Suggs, the lead singer with Madness who would have their first hit record a few months later, and Ian was staying with Suggs's mother when I met him. We discussed Ian's hopes for reforming the band and my hopes for Rock Against Communism, which included plans for future concerts and even perhaps the launching of a new record label.

Ian's plans to reform Skrewdriver proved abortive, at least temporarily, and he returned home to Blackpool three months later. I was, however, forging ahead with plans to hold our first Rock Against Communism concerts. I'd heard that the Young National Front branch in Leeds had held concerts featuring a band called the Dentists and I visited Coventry to see a band called White Boss and to Rugby in Warwickshire to see another band, the name of which escapes me. Finally, in the summer of 1980, we held our first Rock Against Communism concert at Caxton Hall in Red Lion Square, a symbolically significant venue considering that it was here that the anti-NF demonstrator Kevin Gately had been killed during riots at a National Front march six years earlier. The featured bands were White Boss and the Dentists, and several hundred skinheads attended. The music media were apoplectic at the news of the concert whereas I was euphoric that we had finally managed to get Rock Against Communism off the ground.

Skrewdriver, White Boss, and the Dentists were essentially punk bands. I liked punk rock and had bought many records by the first wave of punk groups, including the Ramones, the Sex Pistols, the Stranglers, the Skids, Stiff Little Fingers, and the Angelic Upstarts, but my own musical taste was more eclectic and, quite frankly, more weird. My burgeoning record collection included everything from Glen Miller, Elvis Presley, Buddy Holly, Eddy Cochran, and the Beatles, to modern bands, such as Queen and the aforementioned David Bowie. I even owned some classical music, Wagner (not surprisingly) being my favorite composer. Most of my enthusiasm at this time was, however, reserved for the avant garde, those post-punk bands who were doing strange things with electronics and synthesizers. I bought records by new groups, some of which would later become household names but who were completely unknown beyond a small number of aficionados at the time. These included the Human League, Orchestral Manouevres in the Dark, Tubeway Army, Cabaret Voltaire, Devo, and Ultravox. I saw all of these groups playing live in London as a sort of escapism from my life in politics. I also teamed up with my brother to run what we called a Futurist disco at the Chelsea Drug Store on the fashionable King's Road, a pub which had been immortalized as a den of *chic* iniquity by the Rolling Stones in their 1969 song, "You Can't Always Get What You Want." My name was kept in the background, due to its association with the National Front, and my brother adopted the stage name of Stevo.

Once a week for several months in 1979 and 1980, Steve and I would transport our record collection on the tube from our parents' home in Dagenham to Sloane Square in London's fashionable West End and then carry the records the mile or so down the King's Road to the Drug Store. Upstairs we would play tracks such as "Robots" by Kraftwerk, "I Want to be a Machine" by Ultravox, and "Do the Mussolini Headkick" by Cabaret Voltaire to a small but growing in-crowd of fashionable souls. "Stevo's Futurist Chart" was featured every week in *Sounds*, one of the largest music papers in the country, with the result that my brother began to be sent demo-tapes from weird and wonderful people from all corners of the United Kingdom. We were also sent records to review and I had the secret delight of writing record reviews in my brother's name for the left-wing music media. There was a delicious pleasure in knowing how enraged the editors at *Sounds* would be if they knew that they were publishing my articles. I reviewed an album by an artist called Fad Gadget and another by a group called the Berlin Blondes, employing decadent language as a satirical pastiche and parody of the journal for which I was writing. I recall trying to see how many different forms of psychoses and sexual perversions I could squeeze into one review without my lampooning of the music media becoming too obvious.

Our chic and cliquey time at the Chelsea Drug Store came to an abrupt end after the heavy metal crowd downstairs took a dislike to the weird clientele our music was attracting. Fights broke out, damage was done, and the pub's proprietors shut us down. By this time, however,

Stevo's name was widely known and my brother excelled as an entrepreneur. He founded his own label, Some Bizarre Records, and released a compilation album featuring new bands, three of which, Depeche Mode, Soft Cell, and Blancmange would go on to have hit records. My brother signed a contract with Soft Cell and became the duo's manager. I met Marc Almond, the effeminate half of the duo, when he visited my parent's home. My father was somewhat inebriated, if I recall correctly, and he kept looking at Marc suspiciously, which was not surprising considering that Marc was wearing heavy make-up. Finally, my father inquired whether his guest was male or female, though I don't remember whether the question was a genuine inquiry or a rhetorical question intended as an insult. Evidently Marc took it as the latter because he attacked my father as a fascist and a bigot in his autobiography. I don't believe that I ever met Marc Almond again though I last saw David Ball, the other half of the duo, at my mother's funeral in 2009.

In 1981 Soft Cell had a huge international hit, "Tainted Love," which would top the charts in seventeen countries and would set a Guinness World Record for the longest consecutive stay (forty-three weeks) on the US Billboard Hot 100 chart. At the age of nineteen my brother had become a millionaire and had adopted a jet-set rock-star lifestyle. He and I became estranged as we diverged in terms of lifestyle and philosophy, never really managing to reconcile our multitude of differences.

While my brother was making his fortune in the heady world of global pop music, I was grubbing around in the gutter trying to make headway with Rock Against Communism. Progress had been faltering at best in the wake of the concert at Caxton Hall and I desperately needed some additional help. It came in the form of Ian Stuart's dramatic return at the helm of a revitalized Skrewdriver.

Ian had returned to London in the autumn of 1981, making his home at the Ferndale Hotel on Argyle Square, opposite Kings Cross station. The reformed Skrewdriver released a twelve-inch single, appropriately titled *Back with a Bang*, and contributed two tracks to *United Skins*, a compilation album of songs by the new wave of skinhead bands. In the early months of 1982, as I languished in jail during the first of my two prison sentences, Skrewdriver began to play to packed crowds at the 100 Club on Oxford Street and Skunx in Islington. In May, shortly after my release from jail, I met with Ian Stuart to discuss the possibility of Rock Against Communism concerts and the setting up of an independent record label for skinhead and other Racial Nationalist bands. By the end of the year, a hugely successful RAC concert had been held in Stratford in east London, at which more than five hundred skinheads attended, and White Noise records had been launched.

The first release on the White Noise label was Skrewdriver's *White Power*. Apart from the title track, the two other songs on the record were "Smash the IRA" and the charmingly titled "Shove the Dove." I was at the studio for the recording session and was guest vocalist on "White Power" and "Smash the IRA." In the following months Skrewdriver headlined a series of ever more successful RAC concerts, supported by a new wave of skinhead bands, including Brutal Attack, the Ovaltinies, the Die-Hards, and Peter and the Wolves. In Autumn 1983 Skrewdriver released another single, *Voice of Britain*, the flipside of which, "Sick Society," was a tribute to Albert Mariner, who had been killed the previous May after being struck on the head on his way to a National Front election meeting in Tottenham in north London. In early 1984, *This is White Noise* was released containing tracks by Skrewdriver, Brutal Attack, the Die-Hards, and ABH.

The summer of 1984 saw the first of several Rock Against Communism summer festivals at Nick Griffin's family home in Suffolk, the barn adjacent to the farmhouse being transformed into a makeshift stage. The transformation of this idyllic setting into a heaving mass of skinheads was a sight to behold, though not perhaps a sight for sore eyes. Six bands shared the bill at the festival, indicating the continued growth of RAC, which was now an international phenomenon with skinhead music selling in increasing quantities in Europe and the United States. Encouraged by the burgeoning number of new bands, I decided to rent a recording studio for a week in March 1985 to record the material for a compilation album. I was present for most of the marathon recording session at which eleven bands laid down twenty-two tracks, sixteen of which appeared on the album. Entitled *No Surrender*, the album was released jointly by White Noise and by Rock-o-rama records, a German company, guaranteeing large sales in Europe.

Although these facts highlight the success of Rock Against Communism during the 1980s and show the importance of Skrewdriver to that success, they don't shed any light on the closeness of my friendship with Ian Stuart during this period. It was my custom throughout these years to make my way to the Ferndale Hotel on Friday evenings to meet up with Ian and a few of his closest friends, all of whom were skinheads and most of whom also lived at the hotel. I recall skinheads from Ulster and from Scotland, and also a very pretty Dutch skinhead girl. We would squeeze into Ian's room at around 6pm and the drinking would begin. The choice of beverage was normally hard cider. After a couple of hours we would all walk through the backstreets to a skinhead pub in Islington where the drinking would continue till closing time. On one occasion, my father accompanied me to the Ferndale Hotel and was highly amused to hear some of the skinheads asking each other who the "old geezer" was.

Somehow or other, Ian Stuart and I remained good friends in spite of our political differences. He and I were on different sides in one of the interminable internecine splits that periodically tore the Nationalist movement apart but stayed friends whilst many of our erstwhile comrades were spitting venom at each other. We also remained good friends in spite of the ideological chasm that was beginning to emerge between us. Throughout the period of our friendship, he became more and more aligned with the overt and avowed Nazi elements in the Nationalist movement and wrote songs eulogizing Hitler and the Waffen-SS. During this same period, I was becoming disillusioned with Nazism and found the totalitarianism of the Third Reich increasingly distasteful. I was also becoming more interested in religion, for which Ian had nothing but contempt.

His religion was National Socialism and his god was Hitler.

On December 11, 1985, Ian was sentenced to twelve months in prison for his part in a street brawl between skinheads and a group of black youths. On the following day, I was also sentenced to twelve months in prison, in my case for publishing material likely to incite racial hatred in the pages of *Bulldog*. I saw Ian at Wormwood Scrubs prison on the first morning of my sentence. He was on hotplate duty at breakfast and scooped some porridge into my bowl. We were both subsequently transferred to other prisons and would not meet again until after we were released.

In the latter half of 1986 Ian asked me to write a book on Skrewdriver commemorating the band's tenth anniversary. I was honored to do so as a mark of respect for our friendship. The weeks that I spent writing it was a time of personal confusion as I fought with the dragons of doubt. Even as I documented the history of the band and wrote warmly of our friendship, I doubted my own adherence to the cause that had united us for so many years. The book, which was published as *Skrewdriver: The First Ten Years*, ended with the hope that I would be able "to play my part in Skrewdriver—The Next Ten Years." It was a hollow hope stillborn from the barren womb of an empty heart. The tribute to Skrewdriver would be almost my last political act before my escape into a better world in which sanity is preserved in the pursuit of sanctity. It would be my political swan song, my departing gift to a passing friend.

I met Ian for the last time in 1988 or 1989 after I had dropped out of politics and was making my final approach to the Catholic Church. I traveled by train from my new home in Norwich in eastern England to Ian's new home in Heanor in Derbyshire. From Derby railway station I caught a taxi to the pub in Heanor in which we'd arranged to meet. The taxi driver was an Asian and we began chatting in a friendly fashion. He had recently converted to Christianity and was alive with the zeal of the born again Evangelical. He did not tell me whether he was a convert from Islam, Hinduism, Sikhism, or some other faith but we chatted in a friendly and enthusiastic fashion about our shared discovery of Christ. The ten mile journey took about twenty minutes and by the time we arrived outside the ugly and windowless pub we had struck up quite a convivial rapport. I paid the fare and we departed amicably, wishing each other every blessing. I then crossed the threshold into the gloom of a pub in which all natural light had been exorcised by the boarding up of the windows. It was full of skinheads sporting swastika tattoos and I was struck instantly by the difference in spirit between the affable encounter with the Asian taxi driver and the edginess of my new surroundings. I knew then that I no longer belonged in this world of artificially lit artificial lives. I was amongst old friends but I was nonetheless a stranger.

Ian greeted me with enthusiasm but he seemed out of shape physically and somehow sadder. Later, back at his apartment, when I tried out his dumb-bells, I realized that he was now working out with lighter weights. He was not the bulky hulk that he had once been and I was now clearly stronger than he was. This was a novel experience because Ian had followed a rigorous weight-training regimen in London and was always in better shape than I was. We both noticed the role reversal and I think we were both saddened by it. I caught a wary look in his eye, as though some of the old fire had died. He was not the happy man that he had once been. He was, in fact, a shriveled shadow of the man that he had once been. The image of Gollum in *The Lord of the Rings* came to my mind. We left on friendly terms but the reunion had not been a success. Neither of us ever made the effort to contact the other again.

A few years later I heard that Ian had been killed in a car crash. He was only thirty-six years old. In the wake of his death, he has become a cult figure whose legend has risen phoenix-like from the ashes. This was brought home to me in dramatic fashion when I stumbled across a store rejoicing in the name of the "world famous redneck emporium" in the small town of Laurens, not far from where I now live in South Carolina. My curiosity aroused, I stepped inside and was shocked by what I saw. Pictures of the Ku Klux Klan were on the wall and Nazi insignia was on display throughout the store. There, in pride of place, prominently displayed, was a DVD for sale of "Skrewdriver Live in Germany," on the cover of which was my old friend, screaming into the mike with arm raised in Nazi salute. This sighting of Ian Stuart in a redneck backwater in the Deep South was only a local manifestation of a global phenomenon. A quick surf through cyber-space reveals how he is lauded around the world as a martyr to the cause of the white race. Perhaps, therefore, in death, if not in life, he has won a victory of sorts, though perhaps a pyrrhic one.

Ave et vale, Ian Stuart, or, in the Germanic form that you would no doubt prefer, hail and farewell!

I cannot end this sojourn into the murky world of skinheads and punk rock without recalling another singular act of charity that has stayed in my memory across the decades.

In 1979 I was invited to take part in a debate on immigration on BBC Radio 1, which in the 1970s was the most listened to radio station in the world with audience figures for some shows reaching 20 million. Radio 1's target audience was young people and the station, for the most part, played the latest hits with little or no discussion of any substance in between. The program on which I was invited to participate deviated from the norm by being a talk show in which a small panel of three or four young people would discuss a topic of interest. In the live debate on immigration in which I took part, I had been invited to represent the views of the Young National Front and another guest represented the opposing viewpoint of the Anti-Nazi League. A third "celebrity guest" was Jake Burns, lead singer of the punk band, Stiff Little Fingers. I don't remember much about the debate in the studio beyond the obvious vituperative exchanges between me and the equally acrimonious young person who represented the Anti-Nazi League. The thing that I do remember with palpitating force is the surprise I felt at the kindness with which Jake Burns treated me. I was especially astonished when he invited me to come for a pint or two in a local pub after the show. I was used to being shunned by my adversaries at best, or physically attacked at worst. Being asked to come to the pub for a drink and convivial conversation by one of my opponents was an entirely novel and surprisingly pleasant experience.

There was no doubt that I considered Jake Burns to be an enemy. He and his band Stiff Little Fingers were from Belfast and had a reputation for seeking peace in Northern Ireland at a time when I was preaching total war.* Stiff Little Fingers were also one of the most active bands for Rock Against Racism and had played at the huge RAR Festival in the east end of London in the previous year. In the hate-filled language that I was accustomed to use about such people, he was "scum" or "vermin" whom I would happily have seen dead. Yet, in the face of my own bigotry, Jake Burns sought to befriend me. I was disarmed by this practical act of love and by his gentle persuasiveness in the pub. I wasn't about to be converted to his viewpoint but his example of charity has shone forth as a beacon of goodness across the years. As with the singular act of kindness by the policeman who had lent me the money at the soccer game a year earlier, an act of love speaks louder and longer than any words wasted in argument. Looking back, I now see these moments of charity as lights of clarity that led the way out of the darkness.

---

* Jake Burns was performing with Stiff Little Fingers in Belfast on the night that the UDA leader John McMichael was killed by an IRA bomb (see chapter 11). McMichael's teenage son Gary was at the concert and it was Burns who interrupted the show to announce that Gary McMichael needed to phone home urgently.

CHAPTER 14

POLITICAL PRISONER

ON JANUARY 12, 1982, I was convicted of publishing material likely to incite racial hatred and was sentenced to six months in prison. My hope that an all-white jury would refuse to convict me of offenses under the unpopular Race Relations Act had proved unfounded, though it must be said that the high-stakes gamble had almost paid off. The jury at the first trial in the previous August failed to agree upon a verdict and the conviction at the second trial was only secured by the narrowest of majority verdicts. In the end, after more than four hours of deliberation, the swing vote of one jury member had decided my fate. If he or she had voted the other way, I'd have walked from the courtroom a free man. The government had gained its victory over me but only by the skin of its teeth.

I shouted at the judge as the prison officers dragged me from the courtroom that he was an enemy of the British people and that the day would come when he would face his own judgment. I believed that I was being convicted of a political offense and that I was, therefore, not a criminal but a political prisoner. My defense counsel had made freedom of speech a major part of his case, quoting the famous maxim usually accredited to Voltaire that he might disapprove of what someone said but would defend to the death his right to say it. My counsel also quoted Winston Churchill's insistence that "we sedulously cultivate free speech in this country, even in its most repulsive form." The judge countered that there was no absolute right of free speech, as was evident from the existence of libel laws or laws forbidding the divulging of state secrets.

Surveying the issues raised in the trial more dispassionately from the perspective of the thirty-year chasm that separates me from my angry former self, I still believe that the passing of laws that restrict freedom of speech by the creation of so-called "hate crimes" is a threat to the freedom of everybody, not merely to that of the extremists against whom such laws might initially have been intended. Once governments assign themselves the power to imprison people for saying things that they consider to be "hateful" there is no saying where such powers might lead. In today's meretricious culture it is considered a "hate crime" in some countries to state publicly that homosexual activity is sinful, thereby effectively making the public profession of Christianity illegal. It seems to me that secular fundamentalism is as intolerant as other forms of fundamentalism and that the passing of "hate laws" is an expression of that intolerance. Freedom of speech must include the freedom of those with whom we disagree. If it doesn't it isn't freedom. Ironically I now find myself disagreeing with what my former self said but defending his right to say it. I also find myself echoing the words of Churchill that we must sedulously cultivate free speech, even if it means allowing such freedom to those with whom we disagree strongly. Accepting these affronts to our own beliefs is the price that such freedom costs.

It is, therefore, not without an element of sympathy that I see my old self in my mind's eye being transported from the Central Criminal Court at the Old Bailey to Chelmsford Prison about forty miles to the east of London. When I arrived there at the beginning of 1982, Chelmsford Prison was designated a young person's institution at which prisoners up to the age of twenty-one were incarcerated. Three years earlier it had been the location for *Porridge: The Movie*, a full-length feature film based upon the popular British sitcom. As a consequence, those wishing to see inside the walls of Chelmsford Prison without going to the trouble of committing a criminal offence can do so by watching the movie.

Upon my arrival, I was placed in solitary confinement in the top security A-wing of the prison. Solitary confinement was normally reserved as a form of punishment for miscreant prisoners so my being placed in such confinement represented a very unusual step on the part of the prison authorities. The reason for my segregation from the bulk of the prisoners on B and C wings was the volatile racial climate amongst the inmates. There were a large number of black prisoners but also a very large number of skinhead prisoners. Tensions were already running high and my presence in the volatile situation might have been a catalyst for racial unrest. I should mention that the high profile court case had made the national headlines so my presence as a prisoner would have been a major talking point amongst the prisoners. Considering that I could have been targeted by black prisoners, I'm sure that my own safety also contributed to the decision to segregate me.

During the first weeks of my sentence I was confined to my cell for twenty-three hours of each day, being allowed out only to "slop out" my latrine bucket in the mornings and evenings and to line up for breakfast, lunch, and dinner, after which I would return to the cell to eat. About half an hour each day was spent walking around in circles in the exercise yard in the company of a handful of other prisoners. On one occasion I began a conversation with a prisoner from Belfast who had been arrested in the National Portrait Gallery in London for slashing a portrait of Princess Diana with a knife. Although he was clearly a supporter of the IRA and therefore my sworn enemy, I felt a strange affinity with him because we were both imprisoned for political offenses. I certainly had much more in common with this person than with those who had been imprisoned for drug offenses or burglary. I felt a bond with this young man, imprisoned for the passionate expression of his political views, and was confused and mortified when I discovered that he had alleged to the prison authorities that I had threatened him with physical violence. The sheer and shameless mendacity of this man's entirely groundless allegations astonished me. It remains indelibly in my memory as an act of ignoble cruelty, a dark counterpoint to the positive memory of the act of charity by that far nobler son of Belfast, Jake Burns.

The worst thing about solitary confinement, and the thing about it that strikes fear into the hearts of most prisoners, is the lack of company, the absence of anyone with whom to share one's thoughts. It is also the fear of being alone and the terror of the silence that accompanies solitude. Most prisoners are scared of solitary confinement because they do not know the comfort and company to be found in books, or, more accurately, the comfort and company to be found in the authors of books. I sometimes quip that most of my best friends are dead but are nonetheless the most delightful and liveliest of company. Authors, long since released from this mortal coil, remain alive in their books. It is due to this delightful company of the dead that I look back with a good deal of fondness to the time that I spent in solitary confinement in Chelmsford Prison. It would be an exaggeration, no doubt, to say that I would rather have been languishing in my cell than at liberty with my friends but it is nonetheless true that I sought and found a good deal of solace in the books from the prison library. I was also permitted unlimited writing material and spent much time in the first weeks of my sentence writing a political tract which I would smuggle out of prison and which would subsequently be published as *Fight for Freedom*.

I discovered a previously unknown asceticism in the hours in which I had only my books or my pen for company and was a little alarmed when I discovered that my comrades in the National Front were protesting about my being kept in solitary confinement. The prospect of sharing a cell with anyone else filled me with dread and my heart sank when, after three weeks alone, I was transferred to a cell on D-wing, which I would share with another prisoner. I can't remember the crime my new cellmate had committed, but I do recall that we had absolutely nothing in common. I don't believe that he had ever read a book of any sort and he seemed to lack any intellectual curiosity. If he spoke at all it was to talk about his car or his girlfriend. It was, therefore, with a great sense of relief that I was transferred to another cell. My new cellmate was much more convivial company. He was serving a life sentence for committing grievous bodily harm to his girlfriend after he discovered her infidelity. I wondered what sort of vicious attack and what sort of injuries had been inflicted to warrant such a harsh sentence. Tact, decorum, and my adherence to the "need to know" principle prevented me from asking him for the gory details.

As my twenty-first birthday approached I began to receive wads of birthday cards from every corner of Britain, most of which contained messages of support. The sympathy of many of the prison officers was evident in the fact that they allowed me to receive a couple of dozen cards a day, in contravention of prison regulations which stipulated that prisoners were only entitled to receive three letters a day. On the morning of my birthday, I was taken from my cell to a vacant room where sacks of mail were emptied on the floor in front of me. There were thousands upon thousands of cards. The ones that had been delivered to my cell were only the tip of the iceberg. Although I couldn't have the cards with me in the cell, my birthday present from the prison authorities was to be left alone for a couple of hours reading through the multitude of greetings from well wishers. The experience was heartening, to say the least, helping to make this one of my most memorable birthdays, though perhaps not the happiest or most enjoyable.

During the months of my imprisonment, my comrades pursued a tireless campaign for my release. They held a march and a rally outside the prison, and a "Free Joe Pearce" graffiti campaign resulted in my name being daubed on walls up and down the country. Bridges above main roads and freeways were specially selected and it was difficult to drive any great distance without seeing a "Free Joe Pearce" slogan. The campaign made me something of a celebrity in the prison, especially amongst the prison officers, many of whom made their sympathies known to me. They would report to me the latest place that a "Free Joe Pearce" slogan had appeared. The campaign also brought a response from our opponents. The most amusing was a humorous addition to a "Free Joe Pearce" slogan on a wall in Liverpool. The amended version read "Free Joe Pearce with Every Packet of Nazipops." A less amusing account of the anti-fascist response to the "Free Joe Pearce" campaign can be read on a Marxist website:

> The case of Joe Pearce is an example of how the Race Relations Act can have the reverse of its intended effect. Pearce was imprisoned for Inciting Racial Hatred by publishing a magazine called *Bulldog*. He instantly became a cause célèbre for the National Front. Loads of graffiti went up everywhere saying "Free Joe Pearce." We spent many evenings going round painting that out, or the more creative anti-fascists would simply add ". . . with every packet of

> nazipops"! Nevertheless, the NF at last had their own martyr and that gave them a real boost. A better solution than imprisonment would have been if he had just suffered a terrible accident.*

Another less than charitable response to the "Free Joe Pearce" campaign was an album track called "Gas Joe Pearce" by a Leeds-based punk band called the Electro-Hippies. The vocals are so fast and frenetic that the line "gas Joe Pearce" is the only audible part of the lyrics.

On May 12, 1982, I was released from prison having served four months of my six month sentence. Apart from the general feeling of elation at being liberated, the only specific memory that I retain from my first hours of freedom is the first pint of micro-brewed ale that I consumed at the Eastbrook pub in Dagenham. Never before had the sheer hoppiness of ale danced so delightfully on my tongue! For a few brief and magical moments hoppiness and happiness became synonymous. I realized then that it is abstinence—as well as absence—that makes the heart grow fonder!

---

* http://libcom.org/book/export/html/13434

CHAPTER 15

SURPRISED BY CHESTERTON

ON MAY 28, 1982, only sixteen days after my release from prison, Pope John Paul II became the first Roman Pontiff to visit the British Isles. As a member of the anti-Catholic Orange Order, I opposed the Pope's visit, arguing that Britain had liberated herself from popery during the Reformation and that the Pope was not welcome in the UK. During my regular visits to Ulster, I had learned a rather tasteless chant, "Two popes gone and the queen lives on, doo-da, doo-da!," sung to the tune of "Camptown Races," which alluded to the deaths of Paul VI and John Paul I in 1978. My militant anti-Catholicism was being compromised, however, by an emerging sympathy with some aspects of Catholicism. I rejoiced at the role that John Paul II was playing in bringing down communist tyranny. His visit to Poland in 1979 had sown the seeds for the founding of the Solidarity trade union in the following year, the rise of which I supported passionately. I had also become an admirer of a number of Catholic writers and intellectuals, including Otto Strasser, G. K. Chesterton, and Hilaire Belloc. I did not approve of their Catholicism, at least not at first, but was enamored of their political and social vision.

I was originally attracted to the radical ideas of Strasser, Chesterton, and Belloc because they represented a genuine alternative to the big government of the socialists and the big business of the multinational capitalists. Although I despised communism and its softer Siamese twin, socialism, I was also opposed to the rise of plutocratic globalism in which organizations such as the World Bank and the International Monetary Fund used their wealth to mould global politics and economics in accordance with their own self-interested agenda. Increasingly I perceived myself as being neither on the left nor the right but as representing a distinct "third position." I resented the allegation of our Trotskyite enemies that my comrades and I were the storm troopers of capitalism. According to Trotskyite dogma, "fascism" was the tool with which big business crushed the workers. Yet I had just been imprisoned by a Conservative government under the leadership of Margaret Thatcher, whereas none of my socialist enemies had been singled out for imprisonment. There was a Race Relations Act, supported by socialists and conservatives alike, which made the incitement of racial hatred a crime but there was no corresponding Class Relations Act making it illegal to incite class hatred. The very idea that my comrades and I were being used by the Conservative government, which routinely banned our demonstrations, to crush the workers was patently absurd.

One positive consequence of my imprisonment was an

accentuation of my mistrust of big government, which I perceived in the Orwellian sense as being Big Brother, the crusher of freedom. Having had the power and weight of the modern State pressed down upon me, depriving me of my liberty, I had no love for totalitarianism. As such, I became less and less sympathetic towards Adolf Hitler and the legacy of the Nazi Party. I began to see that communism and Nazism had a great deal in common. As their names indicate, National Socialism and International Socialism were united in their adherence to socialism, which might be described as the belief that big government is the answer to the big problems facing society. My father's criticism of a communist as one who demands that you be his brother or he'll crack your skull applied equally to the Nazis. I now came to see that Big Brother was essentially the same whether he wore a swastika or a hammer and sickle. I was, therefore, looking for an alternative to the Nazism espoused, at least in private, by some of the National Front's leaders and was ripe for the ideas of Strasser, Chesterton, and Belloc.

When I had first joined the National Front, the term "Strasserite" was employed by some of the NF's leaders as a term of contempt against a group of disaffected NF members who had split from the party a few months earlier. I had no idea what a Strasserite was but was happy enough to toe the party line. If the NF leadership said that Strasserism was bad, so be it. I learned subsequently that a Strasserite was a follower of Gregor and Otto Strasser, two leading members of the Nazi Party who represented a perceived threat to Hitler. Gregor Strasser was amongst those assassinated by Hitler on the Night of the Long Knives in 1934; Otto Strasser had been expelled from the Nazi Party in 1930 and had founded the Black Front (*Schwarze Front*), an anti-Hitler resistance movement.

Otto Strasser was very critical of the rabid anti-Semitism of Nazi leaders, such as Hitler, Goebbels, and Streicher, an anti-racist dimension to his *weltanschauung* towards which I was at first uncomfortably ambivalent. And yet, although I remained a racist, I was nonetheless sympathetic to Strasser's distancing of himself from the shrill bigotry of the Hitlerites. Like Strasser, I knew many people whose racism bordered on the pathological. It was difficult for anybody with a modicum of sanity to feel comfortable in the festering presence of such unbridled and venomous hatred.

As I became increasingly disillusioned with Hitlerism, considering those who idolized Hitler as "Nutzis," I became increasingly interested in the ideas of the Strasser brothers. I read a book about Otto Strasser (*Nemesis?* by Douglas Reed), which was life-changing. This was the book that I was holding when I had my nose broken by the Irishman, in the summer of 1981. I still have it as a prized part of my library, its blood-spattered cover serving as a painful reminder of days gone by. Having devoured *Nemesis?*, I sought other books by and about Otto Strasser. I read Douglas Reed's later book, *Prisoner of Ottawa*, and those books by Strasser himself which had been translated into English, including *Hitler and I*, *Germany Tomorrow*, and *History in My Time*. A short time later, I read a book about the other Strasser, *Gregor Strasser and the Rise of Nazism* by Peter D. Stachura. For several years I became an unabashed disciple of Otto Strasser and was proud to call myself a Strasserite in defiance of the Hitlerites amongst the party's leadership.

In essence, Otto Strasser advocated a political creed which harmonized with what I now know as subsidiarity, a key component of the Catholic Church's social doctrine. This was not really surprising considering that Otto Strasser was raised in a devoutly Catholic family; his father was deeply influenced by Pope Leo XIII's social encyclical, *Rerum novarum*, published in 1891, and one of his brothers became a Benedictine monk.* As a Bavarian, Strasser mistrusted Prussianism and opposed the imposition of Prussia's imperialism on the rest of Germany. Rejecting the idea of one German monolithic super-state, centered on Berlin, he sought instead a loose confederation of largely autonomous German-speaking regions, based upon historical principalities. He was also an agrarian who advocated the strengthening of small family farms through a system of usufruct aimed at preventing the accumulation of agricultural land into the hands of wealthy industrialists or speculators. These ideas awakened my own latent localist, decentralist, and agrarian beliefs, aiding my escape from the intellectual bondage of Nazism. Another book which helped in this regard, and which I read at about the same time as my reading of the books by and about Otto Strasser, was *Make and*

---

* This was Paul Strasser who took the name of Bernard in religion. Joining the Benedictines after serving in the First World War, he was ordained to the priesthood in 1923 and emigrated to the United States in 1940. He is the author of *With Christ Through the Year: The Liturgical Year in Word and Symbol* (1947).

Break with the Nazis by Hermann Rauschning. This book, subtitled "Letters on a conservative revolution," differed in its ideological approach from the radicalism of Strasser, but contained much with which I agreed wholeheartedly. Rauschning's condemnation of "the superficial optimism of the credulous believers in 'progress' as a substitute for religion"* met with my enthusiastic approval but it begged a question that I had not seriously considered and which Rauschning asked: "How could there be any rebirth of our society and civilization without the all-important help of the Christian element?"†

There was certainly no "Christian element" in the annual Otto Strasser birthday parties which were held by me and my friends at the height of the Strasserite fad in the early 1980s. On September 10 each year, in honor of our hero, and in mock emulation of the Hitler birthday parties held each year on April 20 by the Nutzis, we would hold a drunken debauch at which we would sing Ulster Loyalist and Irish Rebel songs, transcending both sides of that murderous political divide in our inebriated revelries. Another favorite song, perversely and ironically enough, was Barry McGuire's *Eve of Destruction*, which we sang with great gusto. The highlight of the annual Strasserfest was the Odin Stomp, a wild and frenetic dance performed to the accompaniment of Wagner's *Ride of the Valkyries.*

Continuing my quest for alternatives to international

---

* Hermann Rauschning, *Make and Break with the Nazis*, London: Secker and Warburg, 1941, pp. 232

† Ibid., p. 233

socialism and multinational capitalism, I discovered the political ideas of G. K. Chesterton and Hilaire Belloc. I believe that the person who was most responsible for leading me in the direction of these two great Catholic writers was Andrew Brons, who, many years later, in 2009, would be elected with Nick Griffin as a Member of the European Parliament for the British National Party. In 1980 Andrew became chairman of the National Front, replacing the neo-Nazi, John Tyndall. He was also a professor of politics at Harrogate College in Yorkshire and became, for a short while, a valued and powerful mentor. It was he who suggested that I should study the distributist ideas of Chesterton and Belloc. Specifically, he suggested that I read Chesterton's book, *The Outline of Sanity*, and an essay entitled "Reflections on a Rotten Apple" in another Chesterton book, *The Well and the Shallows*. Since these volumes were both out of print he directed me to Aidan Mackey, a dealer in used books who specialized in Chesterton and Belloc. Aidan would later become a good friend who helped greatly with the research for my biography of Chesterton.

I devoured *The Outline of Sanity*, agreeing with almost everything that Chesterton said and loving the way that he said it. His personality, full of a vigorous *joie de vivre*, seemed to leap from the page into the intimate presence of the reader. More than thirty years later, I can still remember the thrill that I received when reading Chesterton's political philosophy for the first time. This passage from *The Outline of Sanity*, evoking an idealized once and future England, resonates with me now as it resonated then:

I should maintain that there is a very large element still

in England that would like a return to this simpler sort of England. Some of them understand it better than others, some of them understand themselves better than others; some would be prepared for it as a revolution; some only cling to it very blindly as a tradition; some have never thought of it as anything but a hobby; some have never heard of it and feel it only as a want. But the number of people who would like to get out of the tangle of mere ramifications and communications in the town, and get back nearer to the roots of things, where things are made directly out of nature, I believe to be very large.*

In Chesterton, I had found a new friend who would become the most powerful influence (under grace) on my personal and intellectual development over the following years. Having read *The Outline of Sanity* I began to call myself a "distributist," as well as a Strasserite.

Distributism, the new creed to which I subscribed, is rooted in the principle that the possession of productive property—i.e. land and capital—is an essential guarantor of economic and political freedom. As such, a society in which many people possess such property is freer and more just than a society in which fewer people possess it. In practical terms, this means that an economy comprised of many small businesses is better than an economy comprised of few big businesses. The same principle applied to politics means that a society comprised of many small governments—i.e. revitalized local governments—is more

* G. K. Chesterton, *The Outline of Sanity*, London: Methuen & Co., 1928, p. 123

just than a society comprised of one big government, the latter of which is separated from the needs of local people by its size and its geographical distance from them.

Whereas capitalism concentrates the ownership of property into the hands of a few businessmen, socialism seeks to concentrate its ownership into the hands of the State, which means, in practical terms, handing over the ownership of property from a few businessmen to a few politicians. In both scenarios the people are deprived of the productive property which is the guarantor of their economic and political liberty. Choosing between socialism and capitalism, Chesterton wrote, "is like saying we must choose between all men going into monasteries and a few men having harems"*:

> There is less difference than many suppose between the ideal Socialist system, in which the big businesses are run by the State, and the present Capitalist system, in which the State is run by the big businesses. They are much nearer to each other than either is to my own ideal—of breaking up the big businesses into a multitude of small businesses.†

Little did I know it at the time but the "kernel" of distributism is found in what the Catholic Church has called subsidiarity and in the Church's understanding of the inviolable sanctity of the family. This connection between

---

* Quoted in Maisie Ward, *Gilbert Keith Chesterton*, London: Sheed & Ward, 1944, p. 433

† *Illustrated London News*, Oct. 27, 1928

distributism and the family was highlighted by Chesterton:

> The recognition of the family as the unit of the State is the kernel of Distributism. The insistence on ownership to protect its liberty is the shell. We that are Christians believe that the family has a divine sanction. But any reasonable pagan, if he will work it out, will discover that the family existed before the State and has prior rights; that the State exists only as a collection of families, and that its sole function is to safeguard the rights of each and all of them.*

Despite not being a Christian myself, I had no difficulty agreeing with Chesterton's words. I had learned to despise Big Brother in all his manifestations and was enough of a cultural traditionalist to value the role of the family in society. The idea of strengthening the family by weakening the State was very appealing.

Although *The Outline of Sanity* had been easy to read, in the sense that it dealt with political and economic issues with which I could sympathize, my reading of *The Well and the Shallows* would prove more of a challenge to my political pride and religious prejudice. I had bought it for the solitary essay, "Reflections on a Rotten Apple," which was on page 220 of the book, but I decided to read the book from cover to cover.

The Well and the Shallows was one of Chesterton's last books, published in 1935, the year before he died, and much of the book was a defense of his Catholic faith. There

---

* *G. K.'s Weekly*, Jan. 3, 1935

were six separate essays at the beginning of the book, entitled collectively "My Six Conversions," which outlined the various reasons for Chesterton's embrace of Catholicism. For whatever reason, I devoured these essays with the same enthusiasm with which I devoured Chesterton's political essays. I didn't necessarily agree with everything that Chesterton said but I couldn't help liking the way that he said it. Even more unsettling to my own religious prejudices was the uncomfortable feeling that I wanted to like what Chesterton liked, even if I had always believed that I didn't like it. I have no better way of explaining this strange bond that I had formed with Chesterton than to quote C. S. Lewis's brilliant description of Chesterton's immediate impact upon him when, as a young atheist, he had first read one of Chesterton's books:

> I had never heard of him and had no idea of what he stood for; nor can I quite understand why he made such an immediate conquest of me. It might have been expected that my pessimism, my atheism, and my hatred of sentiment would have made him to me the least congenial of all authors. It would almost seem that Providence, or some "second cause" of a very obscure kind, quite over-rules our previous tastes when It decides to bring two minds together. Liking an author may be as involuntary and improbable as falling in love. I was by now a sufficiently experienced reader to distinguish liking from agreement. I did not need to accept what Chesterton said in order to enjoy it. His humour was of the kind

> which I like best . . . the humour which is not in any way separable from the argument but is rather (as Aristotle would say) the "bloom" on dialectic itself . . . Moreover, strange as it may seem, I liked him for his goodness. I can attribute this taste to myself freely (even at that age) because it was a liking for goodness which had nothing to do with any attempt to be good myself . . . It was a matter of taste: I felt the 'charm' of goodness as a man feels the charm of a woman he has no intention of marrying . . . In reading Chesterton . . . I did not know what I was letting myself in for. A young man who wishes to remain a sound Atheist cannot be too careful of his reading.*

Lewis was nineteen-years-old when he first read Chesterton, about the same age that I was when I read *The Outline of Sanity* and *The Well and the Shallows*, and our reactions to Chesterton were exactly the same. I was as mystified as Lewis at the way that Chesterton had made an immediate conquest of me. Like Lewis, it might have been expected that my own anti-Catholicism would have made Chesterton the least congenial of authors. Yet, as with Lewis, it was almost as though something mystical or providential had brought together our two minds in friendship. It was indeed like falling in love. I had fallen in love with the wit and wisdom of Chesterton and had fallen under the charm of his humor and humility. Like Lewis, I did not know what I was letting myself in for. A young atheist cannot be too careful of his reading, nor can

---

* C. S. Lewis, *Surprised by Joy*, London: Fount, 1998, pp. 147-48

a young racist anti-Catholic. In reading Chesterton I was undermining my own most dearly held prejudices. Lewis believed that "Chesterton had more sense than all the other moderns put together"—except, of course, for his Christianity. I believed that Chesterton had more common sense than anyone else—except, of course, for his Catholicism and his anti-racism.

I realize now what I had no way of realizing then, that it was the combination of Chesterton's eminently rational mind and his transparently virtuous heart that had captured and captivated me. It was the same charm of goodness that I had witnessed in the policeman who had lent me money and the punk rocker from Belfast who had invited me—his enemy—to the pub. It was the presence of goodness, the light of sanctity shining forth in the darkness, the life of love that can kill all hatred.

CHAPTER 16

BELLOC, LEWIS, AND OTHER GOOD INFLUENCES

SHORTLY AFTER I finished reading Chesterton's *The Well and the Shallows* a Jehovah's Witness knocked on the door of my house in south London. Normally I would have done whatever was necessary to induce these intrusive proselytizers to leave. On this occasion, however, I decided to indulge in an enjoyable intellectual exercise. I pretended that I was a Catholic and set about using Chesterton's arguments for the Faith in my discussion with the visitor on my doorstep. I had great fun putting myself in the shoes of a papist and was convinced by the end of our discussion that I had won the argument. The Jehovah's Witness was, however, not convinced, thereby depriving me of the strange satisfaction of converting someone to a creed in which I did not myself believe. Looking back on this episode, I nurture the quixotic hope that I had perhaps sowed a few seeds of doubt in my interlocutor's mind about the false creed in which he believed so fervently; more importantly, I hope that I had also planted seeds of faith in the ancient creed which he had argued against.

I had paid the princely sum of £12 for my copy of *The Well and the Shallows* due to its being a first edition with its original dust jacket. It was, however, very easy in those days to pick up Chesterton books in used bookstores for around 20 pence. Chesterton's star had faded in the culture of liberalism that prevailed in the wake of the Second Vatican Council and few people seemed interested in his robust apologetics. Although times have changed and Chesterton is once again very much en vogue, I am happy to have built my extensive library of Chesterton titles at so little cost. I had very little money and I doubt that I could have indulged my Chesterton habit so liberally had the cost of his books been much higher.

I spent many happy hours trawling through used bookstores, of which there were many in those more literate times, buying anything by Chesterton and also anything by his great friend and comrade in arms, Hilaire Belloc. Chesterton acknowledged that Belloc was the founder of distributism, of whom Chesterton considered himself a disciple, and Belloc's *Servile State* and his *Essay on the Restoration of Property* were seminal works which demanded a place in any self-respecting distributist's library. I devoured these books with the same devotion with which I devoured the works of Chesterton. Furthermore, I developed a literary friendship and ideological affinity with Belloc, which was second only to my love of Chesterton in intensity. I read many books by Belloc during this period and his *Four Men* became and has remained one of my all-time favorite works, transporting me into a Shire every bit as arcane and Arcadian as that to be found in Middle-earth.

Another important and beneficent influence that the reading of Chesterton and Belloc had upon me was a weakening of the Prussophilia that I had inherited at my father's knee. Through my sympathy with Strasser's Bavarian perspective, I had already begun to distinguish between Prussia and Germany, the former of which I now perceived to represent a belligerent and destructive imperialism. In reading Belloc and Chesterton, I came to see European history through their anti-Prussian eyes and with their Francophile perspective. My sympathies swung from Germany to France, freeing me further from my previous ideological bondage to the Teutonic and Norse fetish. In Belloc's view—adopted and echoed by Chesterton—France had always been at the heart of Christendom, whereas the Germanic spirit had always been on the heretical hinterlands and barbaric fringes, threatening European civilization with its uncivilized presence. I have since come to see that Belloc's own Francophile perspective suffers from patriotic bias and that his and Chesterton's sympathy for the French Revolution and the secular Republic that followed in its wake is untenable and indefensible from an orthodox Christian perspective. At the time, however, the psychologically seismic shift from Germany to France was a vital move in the right direction, leading me away from all that is indubitably evil in the pride of Prussia and in its genocidal legacy.

Closer to home, my reading of Chesterton and Belloc caused me to reconsider the nature of my love for my own country and, more radically, to ask fundamental questions about which country it was to which I owed allegiance. I had been brought up by my father to love Britain and the

British Empire and to rejoice in great British military victories, such as Trafalgar, Waterloo, Rorke's Drift, and the Battle of Britain. No real distinction was made between "Britain" and "England," so that the English victory at Agincourt was mentioned in the same breath as the aforementioned British victories. England and Britain were certainly not synonymous in Chesterton's eyes. On the contrary, Chesterton seemed to owe his allegiance to the one and not particularly to the other. He was an Englishman who looked upon the Scots, Irish, and Welsh as being distinctly different peoples, no more English than were the French or the Germans. He taught me the difference between being a Little Englander and a Great Britisher, the former of which rejoices in the smallness of his country and its uniqueness, whilst the latter rejoices in its greatness and the extent to which it has expanded and implanted its influence around the world. A Little Englander was a nationalist, in the diminutive sense of the word; he merely wished for autonomy for England in the same way that a Welsh, Irish, or Scottish nationalist sought autonomy for their respective nations. A Great Britisher was not a nationalist in this healthy sense of the word but was an imperialist who sought to impose his will on other nations. Far from being a nationalist, a Great Britisher was an internationalist who sought to bring other nations under the British imperial yoke. In coming to understand and sympathize with Belloc's and Chesterton's opposition to the Boer War, I came to see that the power of the British Empire was that of a big bully, fighting at the behest of plutocratic mining interests to subjugate the legitimate aspirations of the Afrikaans farmers. I also began to feel ambivalent towards the concept of "Britain" because of the British Nationality Act of 1948 which had bestowed British citizenship on people from the Indian sub-continent and from the Caribbean, thereby opening the floodgates of immigration. Although the official party line of the National Front was that non-whites could not be "British," it was clearly the case that the rise of the Empire had also given rise to the cosmopolitanism that led to immigration. Slowly but surely, under the benign influence of Chesterton and Belloc, I metamorphosed from being a Great Britisher to being a Little Englander. Many years later, I endeavored to summarize the difference between the two in a short poem:

When Britain had an Empire
The sun would never set,
But the sun set over England
And Englishmen forget
That greater than the Empire
Are the rolling Yorkshire moors,
And more glorious the Dales
Than all the Empire's wars.

As I delved deeper into distributism I became increasingly aware that it was a manifestation of the social teaching of the Catholic Church. Belloc and Chesterton were merely the propagators and popularizers of the Church's social doctrine as expounded by Pope Leo XIII in *Rerum novarum* (1891), a doctrine that would later be restated, reconfirmed, and reinforced by Pope Pius XI in *Quadragesimo anno* (1931), by John Paul II in *Centesimus annus*

(1991), and by Benedict XVI in *Caritas in veritate* (2009). It was from *Rerum novarum* that Belloc had drawn his ideas and inspiration on political and economic issues, although his later writings, most particularly his *Essay on the Restoration of Property* (1936), would have been able to draw inspiration from *Quadragesimo anno* as well. Aware of this connection between the distributism that I now espoused and the teaching of the Catholic Church, I made a point of reading *Rerum novarum* and *Quadragesimo anno*, which I very much enjoyed. I was also pleased, whilst browsing in a used bookstore in Streatham in south London, to come across Pius XI's encyclical *Divini redemptoris* (1937), his famous attack "on atheistic communism." Against my will, I found myself being attracted to the papacy as a clear voice of wisdom in a muddled world, further stimulating my embryonic attraction to the Church.

It was at around this time that Nick Griffin introduced me to *Small is Beautiful* by the German economist, E. F. Schumacher, a work, both popular and profound, which almost single-handedly redefined the public perception of economics and its impact upon the human person and his environment. In practical terms Schumacher counteracted the idolatry of giantism with the beauty of smallness. People, he argued, could only feel at home in human-scale environments, of which the family was the archetype. His insistence that the question of scale in economic life should not—and, indeed, morally speaking, could not—be separated from the overriding dignity of the human person, shifted the whole focus of economic thought away from impersonal market forces and back to the dignity of human life. I embraced Schumacher as another mentor whom I could trust and was astonished, years later, to discover that he had become a Catholic in 1971, two years before his bestselling book was published, and that the social teaching of the Catholic Church had been a major part of his own thinking.

Nick Griffin also introduced me to the works of John Seymour, author of *The Complete Guide to Self-Sufficiency*, a best-seller when first published in 1976. Seymour is best described as England's own Wendell Berry, an advocate of self-sufficiency and a tireless critic of modern consumerism and materialism. Seymour's rhetorical broadside against modernity, *Bring Me My Bow*, was hugely influential upon my development and is still a treasured part of my library. Seymour opposed big government and stated that Suffolk, the county in which he was living at the time and the one in which I had spent the halcyon days of my childhood, was as large as any nation should be, suggesting that even the littleness of England was too large for human-scale government. This harmonized with Belloc's waxing lyrical about his own county of Sussex in *The Four Men*, accentuating what I would later come to see as the theology of place. This concept, which is truly at the heart of Seymour's and Belloc's work, is quintessentially incarnational: the sense of "place" is linked to the love of home, and the love of home is itself salted by the home's temporary absence or unattainability. Paradoxically it is the sense of exile that gives the love of home its intensity and power. It is expressed most sublimely in the *Salve Regina*, in which the "poor banished children of Eve," lost in "this vale of tears," hope that, "after this our exile," we might behold the Blessed Fruit of our Mother's womb, Jesus. Heaven is our haven, Jesus is our home. One's earthly home, or "native place," is "the shell of one's soul," as Belloc described it in *The Path to Rome*, because it is an incarnated inkling of the home for which we are made and toward which we are mystically directed. This theology of place is an almost omnipresent theme in Belloc's work. Few writers have felt so intensely the sense of exile, and hence the love of home, to the degree that Belloc did. In his love of Sussex at the heart of *The Four Men* and in poems such as "Ha'nacker Mill" or "The South Country," Belloc's work resonates with the love of earth as a foreshadowing of the love of heaven. It is in this soil-soul nexus that the nub of Belloc's profundity is to be discovered. It manifests itself in the tension between permanence and mutability, and finds infectious expression in the perfect balance between wistfulness and whimsy that Belloc achieves. I felt intensely this soil-soul nexus, though I did not yet perceive it in the theological terms of seeking a mystical union between the heart and the hearth.

During another of my habitual expeditions into used bookstores my eyes settled on a book called *Surprised by Joy* by someone called C. S. Lewis. I had heard of C. S. Lewis, possibly as the author of *The Lion, the Witch and the Wardrobe*, a book I'd never read, but I knew nothing about him. Perhaps I had read somewhere that he was a Christian writer. Perhaps not. The shadow of the years has descended upon the surface of my memory. Either way, something prompted me to take the book from the shelf. Flicking through the pages I came across the passage about

Lewis's first reading of Chesterton. As my eyes read Lewis's words, my heart leapt, surprised by the joy of discovering a kindred spirit. It was uncanny that someone in a field hospital in France, during the First World War, more than sixty years earlier, could have felt exactly the same way that I had upon discovering Chesterton. I purchased the book and added Lewis as another of my mentors. From now on, when trawling through the treasures in used bookstores, I would search for titles by Lewis as well as those by Chesterton and Belloc.

In reading Lewis's *Mere Christianity*, as in reading Chesterton's *Orthodoxy*, I learned that the Christian creed might possibly provide the very credentials for truth itself. In reading Lewis's *The Problem of Pain*, as in reading Chesterton's *The Man Who was Thursday*, I began to perceive the sense to be found in suffering, and in reading *A Grief Observed* I saw the abstract arguments about suffering become incarnate in Lewis's own pain at losing his wife. In Narnia, as in Chesterton's *Manalive* and his Father Brown stories, I discovered the wonder of remaining child-like, and the wisdom that springs from this wonder-filled innocence. And, of course, in Lewis, as in Chesterton, there was so much more to discover. Finally, through their guidance, and like John in *The Pilgrim's Regress*, I would lay myself at the feet of Mother Kirk. In reading the works of Lewis and Chesterton, and in the enjoyment of their company, I had unknowingly crossed the threshold of hope and had entered Aslan's country.

These observations are, however, the fruit of experience perceived with the wisdom of hindsight. At the time, back in the 1980s, I was unaware of crossing any such threshold. I was still very much embroiled in the racist politics of the National Front, living a double-life in which I wrote hate-filled propaganda during the day and read the love-filled pages of Chesterton and Lewis at night. I was not aware of any contradiction, at least at first, and sought to bring the two warring viewpoints together by a process of Orwellian doublethink, which is defined in *Nineteen Eighty-four* as "the power of holding two contradictory beliefs in one's mind simultaneously, and accepting both of them."* Throughout the early to mid-eighties I became very adept at doublethink, endeavoring to squeeze the square peg of my Christian reading into the round hole of my racist ideology. As my knowledge of Christianity grew larger and my commitment to racial nationalism diminished in consequence, the strain of squeezing an ever larger peg into an ever-shrinking hole would eventually become impossible. My days of doublethink were numbered. To switch metaphors, my position was like that of the frog in the pan of cold water that is being heated slowly and imperceptibly. The frog is boiled alive, not realizing it until it is too late. In similar fashion, I was in a cauldron of Christian influences which was coming slowly to the boil. I was being converted without realizing it.

---

* George Orwell, *Nineteen Eighty-four*, London: Secker & Warburg, 1949, p. 32

CHAPTER 17

CAPTAIN TRUTH

EVEN AS Chesterton, Belloc and Lewis were working their unseen and grace-filled magic, enlightening my mind and healing my heart imperceptibly, I continued to pursue the paths of radical politics as if nothing was changing. Following my release from prison in May 1982 I resumed my editorship of *Bulldog* under the alias of Captain Truth. Although I was willing to go back to prison, I was in no hurry to do so and the adoption of this pseudonym or *nom de guerre* was intended to make it more difficult for the government to prosecute me a second time under the Race Relations Act.

Apart from my editorship of *Bulldog*, I continued to edit *Nationalism Today*, which became the voice of the radical or Strasserite element in the National Front. My Strasserite comrades and I began to exert an increasing influence within the party, aided and abetted by the growth of the Young National Front of which I remained chairman. In December 1983 a Strasserite coup effectively placed the radical element in charge of the party, placing the leadership into the hands of young men who were mostly in their early to mid-twenties. This lack of maturity would soon manifest itself in a pathetic descent into internecine feuding, ideological name-calling, Machiavellian backstabbing, and the sort of juvenile radicalism that is rightly the target of satire. For a brief honeymoon period, however, the Strasserites ruled the radical roost. Seeking to put our principles into practice, we adopted an anti-American stance, calling for British withdrawal from NATO and the removal of all US military bases from Britain. I took part in a "Yanks Go Home" protest outside the Lakenheath airbase in Suffolk, during which we chanted anti-American slogans and brandished placards at those entering and leaving the base. Some of our members became embroiled in a fight in a local pub with members of the US Air Force but on this occasion I was not physically involved.

Shortly after my release from prison I became involved in a relationship which resulted in an unexpected pregnancy. Abortion was seriously discussed and, to my lasting shame, it was I, more than the child's mother,* who favored this "choice." Thankfully the baby, my daughter Lorna, was allowed to be born and a little over eighteen months later a second child, Joe, was born. My relationship with their mother was turbulent and tortuous, burning into my conscience and consciousness the disastrous nature of heedless and headless passion. As with all self-centered relationships, the partners in crime make their own lives hell and,

* I am referring to the mother of Lorna and Joe in this impersonal manner to preserve her privacy and anonymity. This should not be taken as being indicative of any sense of bitterness on my part.

far more tragically, they also make the lives of their children a living hell. I remember my efforts to be reunited with my children after their mother had disappeared with them. Joe was a baby and Lorna was probably around two-years-old. When I was eventually allowed to see them again, I could see the horrible suffering that the so-called tug-of-love between her parents had inflicted on our daughter. As I drove her home, she was clearly distressed, thumb in mouth, staring out of the window of the car in bewildered and hurt confusion. It is always the children who suffer from sexual licentiousness, either those whose lives are terminated in the womb or those whose lives are brutalized by the selfishness of their parents. Children are the voiceless victims of sexual immorality.

I could say much more about this episode in my life but I'm concerned to protect the privacy of those I love. In any event, I am not writing a biography but a conversion story. From a biographical perspective my children play an important and integral role in the entirety of my life, but from the perspective of the journey from racial hatred to rational love their role, though very poignant and important, can be explained in relatively few words. I learned from the recklessness of my youthful relationships that unbridled passion is destructive and brings neither happiness nor satisfaction. On the contrary, it brings suffering to all concerned. I also learned that the feelings that lead to such relationships have nothing whatever to do with love. Selfishness is never love. The mistakes of my youth have allowed me to see what true love is through the experience of its absence. They have allowed me to see that love is not a feeling but an action. It is the laying down of one's life for the beloved. It is not the laying down of someone else's life or body for our own gratification. Ultimately, as a Christian, I have come to see that love is not merely an action but a commandment. We are commanded to love the Lord our God and to love our neighbor—and our enemy. Clearly true love has nothing to do with selfishness in any of its guises. It is the giving of ourselves to others.

Amidst the turbulent selfishness of my private life, an act of true love from an unexpected source, an avowed enemy, would lead me closer to an understanding of love's self-sacrificial heart. The enemy in question was a leading member of the National Council for Civil Liberties, the British equivalent of the ACLU, with whom I had met to discuss an egregious breach of the civil liberties of National Front members during a demonstration in the north of England. I had been angered when a convoy of National Front buses, destined for a march near Manchester, was stopped by the police. I had been angered still further when the police imprisoned the several hundred NF members, including a number of infirm elderly people, for several hours. There were no toilet facilities on the buses and the police refused to allow people to leave the vehicles to answer the call of nature. The resulting discomfort was tantamount to torture! The police had no legal right to behave in such a fashion and I was determined to seek redress for their breaking of the law.

It was with this in mind that I went to the offices of the NCCL and asked to speak with one of their legal advisers. In truth, I did not expect any help but wanted to prove that the NCCL was a hypocritical organization which only believed in assisting those who shared its own socialist or libertarian agenda. I was met by a Jewish American, which inflamed my anti-Semitic and anti-American prejudices.* Explaining to him the breach of civil liberties that my comrades and I had suffered, I expected to see him squirm on his seat as he endeavored to explain why he was unwilling to assist "fascists" or "Nazis." This would have enabled me to take the moral high ground and denounce him as a hypocrite. It would also have made a great story in one of the National Front's publications, proving that the NCCL was not really interested in civil liberty for everyone but was only a front for socialist agitation. Imagine my surprise when my interlocutor listened sympathetically to my complaints and promised to help. Here was a man of principle, a Jew, my sworn enemy, who disagreed with my political views but was willing to fight for my right to express them. As events transpired he was overruled by the hypocrites with whom he worked, proving my suspicions correct about the NCCL. Imagine my further surprise, indeed astonishment, when this Jewish American resigned his position with the NCCL in protest, showing me the meaning of love in his act of self-sacrifice on behalf of his enemy. Once again, as with my earlier encounters with the punk rocker and the policeman, an act of love shone forth as a beacon of truth in the darkness of my life, lighting the way to a destination of which I was as yet unaware.

* Alas, I cannot remember his name.

My efforts to seek redress for the abuse of police powers were indicative of an increased awareness of the Orwellian tactics that the police were using. It was widely believed that the National Front was beset by police informers and I had little doubt that my home phone number was tapped. My worst fears about the nature of police surveillance were confirmed when a friend of mine, a member of the police force, was summoned to a meeting at Scotland Yard at which he was shown photographs of himself in various London pubs in my company. He was told to resign from the police or else face dismissal proceedings. The affair illustrated that I was being followed and surreptitiously photographed and that my activities were being closely monitored. The experience of the weight of Big Brother's presence solidified my own disdain for the very notion of the police state, thereby distancing me still further from fascism and its belief in big government. It also accentuated the desire for a libertarian, distributist, or subsidiarist approach to politics in which the rights of individuals and families would be protected from the encroachment of centralized government.

Some time in 1985 I was awakened in the middle of the night by a loud knock on the door. Bleary-eyed, I found myself confronted by a number of police officers armed with a search warrant. They pushed past me and commenced a thorough search for evidence that I was in fact the elusive Captain Truth. I had never contemplated the possibility of a police raid, believing in my naïveté that my home was sacrosanct and beyond the reach of the state. As such, the evidence of my continuing editorship of *Bulldog* was soon discovered. I was charged once again under the Race Relations Act with publishing material deemed likely to incite racial hatred. On December 12, 1985, I was found guilty and sentenced to twelve months in prison.

CHAPTER 18

A SECOND PRISON SENTENCE

THE FIRST couple of days of the second prison sentence were perhaps the darkest of my life. Broken in spirit and troubled in mind, I was painfully aware that I was not the brave and brazen political soldier who had gone to prison four years earlier. Filled with doubt and uncertainty, and unconvinced of my own convictions, I seemed to be a mere shadow of my former self. And yet my former self was not what it seemed. It was only a shadow of the real self, the latter of which had always been overshadowed by pride and prejudice, depriving itself of the light that it needed to grow.

Something was happening to me. In the darkest depths of my desolation, the smallest of candles was being lit. Amidst the ruins of my old life the seeds of a new life were germinating. Imperceptibly, my faith in race and nation was being sapped by my embryonic faith in Christ and His Church, a faith which was in gestation, not fully formed but continuing to grow, deep inside, with every passing day. This embryonic faith would manifest itself in a surprising way on the very first day of my sentence.

Upon my arrival at Wormwood Scrubs prison, somewhat shell shocked, I was asked all the customary questions that a new prisoner is asked. Was I an alcoholic? Did I use drugs? Did I have certain diseases? What was my religion? The last question took me by surprise. I hesitated for a moment and then replied that I was a Catholic. I couldn't believe what I had just said. Much to my astonishment, I had unthinkingly made my first profession of faith in a creed that I did not properly understand. I was not a Catholic, of course, so my answer was not strictly honest. Yet I was more of a Catholic than anything else. I was certainly not an Anglican in anything but the technical sense of having been christened as a baby in an Anglican church. If anything, I now considered the Church of England worthy of contempt, my reading of Chesterton and Belloc having awakened in me the sobering realization that the Anglican Church had been founded on the loins of Henry VIII. Nor was I an agnostic, or, if I was, I didn't want to be. I wanted answers whereas agnostics didn't even care about the questions. I was no longer satisfied with the pathetic and apathetic no-man's-land of religious indifference.

What on earth or in heaven was I? Was I anything? Wasn't I best defined not so much by what I was but by what I wasn't? I wasn't an Anglican, except on a technicality; I wasn't an agnostic except begrudgingly; I wasn't a Catholic except that I wanted to be.

No, I wasn't a Catholic . . . but I wanted to be . . .

My unexpected answer to the unexpected question had been a baptism of desire.

A day or so later I had the mystical encounter with the rosary with which this account of my spiritual odyssey began. Opening my heart and mind in prayer for the first time, it seemed that the floodgates of grace were unloosed and that the inner sanctum of my being was being washed clean of the dirt and detritus of a life ill-lived. I was still a miserable sinner and I was still in miserable ignorance of the faith to which I had declared my allegiance but the seeds of desire were being watered and the flower of faith was beginning to grow.

After a few days at Wormwood Scrubs I was transferred to Standford Hill prison on the Isle of Sheppey in Kent where I would spend the remainder of my sentence in solitary confinement. As with the first sentence, I took to the life of solitude with relative ease. This time, however, I would spend almost six months in solitary confinement, compared with only the first three weeks of the earlier sentence. I was allowed out of my cell each day to clean the toilets and showers in the punishment block and also, on occasion, to scrape several layers of varnish from the floor of the officers' mess. The toilet cleaning was an almost pleasurable experience in relation to the laborious and painstaking chore of removing the layers of varnish with a tiny and inadequate scraping implement. After several hours of grueling and blister-forming effort only a few square feet of floor would be varnish-free. It could be likened to scrubbing the floor with a toothbrush—only much slower and much more painful!

Life alone in the cell was centered on daily routines that became ritualistic. The tuning in to radio shows and the time set aside for reading and physical exercise were each assigned certain portions of the day. Deviation from this daily ritual was rare and was usually accompanied by a demoralizing disorientation. An unforeseen benefit of my solitary existence was the overcoming of my childhood arachnophobia. In the absence of human contact, the spiders in my cell became pets. They were companions in solitude. There was one particularly large spider which lived in the space between a table and the wall of the cell. During the day it would not move from its woven den. At night it would stand in the middle of the floor of the cell, scampering for cover as soon as the light was switched on. Another smaller spider had a very different lifestyle, perambulating around the cell at all times of the day and night so that one never knew when or where it might be seen. It was odd how much I missed this wandering friend when he ceased to make his unexpected visits.

As with the previous imprisonment, my time in solitary confinement afforded a great deal of time for reading. I devoured dozens of books during the months of solitude. I read Newman's *Apologia* and his novel *Loss and Gain* and also *Là Bas*, a luridly spiritual novel by Joris-Karl Huysmans. I also read Cardinal Mindszenty's *Memoirs*, feeling an affinity with him as a political prisoner and as a victim of communism. I read several Chesterton books, confirming my admiration for this most convivial of companions, and, most important, I wandered into Middle-earth, experiencing its magic and majesty for the first time. What can one possibly say about one's first reading of *The Lord of the Rings*? I had been intending to read it for years but its magisterial length had always deterred me. Now, with time in abundance and distractions at a minimum, I followed Frodo on his quest, accompanying him with a sense of wonder and awe. I didn't grasp the full depth of meaning in the story and had no idea on that first reading of the extent to which, as Tolkien insisted, *The Lord of the Rings* is "a fundamentally religious and Catholic work."* I knew, however, that Tolkien was a Catholic, like almost every other writer whom I admired, and I sensed that only a Catholic could write something as utterly good, true, and beautiful as *The Lord of the Rings*.

Another book I plucked from the prison library was *The Man Who Gave His Company Away*, a biography of Ernest Bader, founder of the Scott Bader Commonwealth. It is the story of a successful businessman who decided to give his company to his employees by turning it into a producer's cooperative. Most people believed that Bader's quixotic action would presage disaster for the company but, contrary to all skeptical expectations, the Scott Bader Commonwealth prospered. I was moved to sympathy for Bader, a practicing Christian, because his beliefs harmonized with the distributism of Chesterton and Belloc and with the subsidiarist principles of the Catholic Church. Years later, gathering research for my book, *Small is Still Beautiful*, I visited the Scott Bader Commonwealth. I was pleasantly surprised to discover that it had not only continued to prosper in a very competitive market but that it was

* Humphrey Carpenter, ed., *The Letters of J. R. R. Tolkien*, Boston/New York: Houghton Mifflin, 2000, p. 172

virtually the only small or medium sized company in the polymer industry that had not gone bankrupt or been swallowed up by the huge multinationals. The edifying irony is that Bader's company had survived because he had given it away. If he had not done so it would have long since ceased to exist.

Two crucially important books which I read at this time were *Apologetics and Catholic Doctrine* by Archbishop Sheehan and *Aquinas* by F. C. Copleston. The first was a superb introduction to Catholic philosophy and theology, the second a succinctly lucid introduction to the thought of St. Thomas Aquinas by a brilliant Jesuit scholar. Reading these books opened my eyes to the inextricable connection between faith and reason, convincing me of the rational rectitude of Catholic doctrine.

In sharp contrast to the sanity and sanctity of the great minds I was meeting in the pages of the books I was reading, my old friends in the National Front were once again at each other's throats in the latest bout of internecine feuding. My closest friends had become sworn enemies of each other and I was horrified and sickened by the outright lies being disseminated and by the merciless character assassination being perpetrated. How could people who had been the best of friends become so spiteful towards each other? I was especially sickened by a scurrilous booklet produced by Nick Griffin and his allies which disseminated outrageous lies against those whom Nick had previously called his friends. The "facts" published in this booklet were so poisonous that I found it hard to believe that my friend could have been capable of such gutter-scraping mendacity.

Indeed it beggared belief. There were only two possible explanations. Either he had gone quite mad and really believed the "facts" or else he was a cold-blooded and cynical Machiavel who would stop at nothing to gain power within the Party. Firmly believing in Lord Acton's maxim that power tends to corrupt and that absolute power tends to corrupt absolutely, I wondered what horrors these people would perpetrate if they ever got their hands on any real power. If they could assassinate their friends so cynically with words what would they do to their enemies if they ever had the power of the State behind them? The thought sent shivers up my spine.

Increasingly disillusioned with the ideology of the National Front and feeling betrayed by those whom I thought were my friends, I resolved to resign from politics as soon as I was released from prison.

CHAPTER 19

THE GUTTER AND THE STARS

We are all in the gutter, but some
of us are looking at the stars.

—Oscar Wilde

I WALKED free from Standford Hill prison on June 12, 1986.

Oh, what a glorious day that was! There is a sense of liberation, truly ecstatic, which only the release from prison can bestow. There is nothing like it. Without experiencing the misery of incarceration it is impossible to reach the sheer ecstasy of freedom, the exquisite delight of release. Once experienced, this feeling is never forgotten. It stays with one as a memory of bliss, a fading light of joy amidst the mundane shadows of life. It is, however, and as I have come to understand, not merely a shadow of the past but a foreshadowing of the future. It is an inkling of that greater ecstasy which awaits the release of the soul from mortal life's purgatorial prison into the fullness of freedom to be found in Paradise.

Unfortunately, and in spite of my initial resolve, it would prove much more difficult to liberate myself from the prison of politics. I was imprisoned by my own past. I had been involved in politics for the past ten years, since the age of fifteen, and I didn't know anybody who was not a political activist. I had worked full time for the National Front for the previous eight years. I had lived and breathed nothing but radical politics for so long that I didn't know anything about life beyond its walls.

I did make an effort to escape, retreating to a wonderfully peaceful house, called Fisherman's Cottage, in the sleepy seaside town of Kessingland on the Suffolk coast. I lived on the second floor, overlooking a garden in which rabbits grazed all day long. Just beyond, a stone's throw from the house, was the sandy beach and the rolling waves of the North Sea. It was summer and I would sleep with my bedroom window open. Every night I would be lulled to sleep by the lullaby of waves caressing the shore. Every morning I would awake to see the sun rising over the sea's horizon. Every Sunday I would walk the five miles to Lowestoft, along the cliff top, with the sea below me on my right, to Our Lady, Star of the Sea, the nearest Catholic church. As the liturgy swept over me, I found true peace and healing, a salve for the soul and solace for my worn and torn spirit. I remember particularly the way that my heart was lifted with delight by the recessional hymn, "Hail, Queen of Heaven, the Ocean Star," which seemed to be sung most weeks:

> Hail, Queen of heav'n, the ocean star,
> Guide of the wand'rer here below;
> Thrown on life's surge, we claim thy care:

Save us from peril and from woe.
Mother of Christ, star of the sea,
Pray for the wand'rer, pray for me.

O gentle, chaste, and spotless maid,
We sinners make our prayers through thee;
Remind thy son that he has paid
The price of our iniquity.
Virgin most pure, star of the sea,
Pray for the sinner, pray for me.

Little did I know that this time of peace and healing was merely the calm before the renewal of the storm. I was visited by an old friend and comrade, whose mission was to induce me to return to the political fray. I refused resolutely, explaining that the betrayal of old and trusted friends had taken the wind from my sails and that I no longer had the heart to fight, least of all to fight a civil war against my own erstwhile comrades. My friend, whom I loved dearly, looking broken and dejected, went for a walk. Sometime later I saw him from my window. He was sitting on the beach, crest-fallen, throwing stones into the waves. My heart went out to him. I felt angry at those former friends who had made him the victim of calumny. I began to see my withdrawal from politics as a sin of omission. In failing to take a stand I was condemning the innocent to defeat. I felt called to use the influence that I had within the movement to seek justice for the victims of lies and libel. I became convinced that I was duty-bound to champion my friends against the Machiavellian dragon that had seized control of the National Front. It seemed that justice demanded that

I take up the cudgels against the perpetrators of injustice, which meant fighting against some of my closest friends, not least of whom was Nick Griffin. I had no heart for the fight but neither did I have the heart to refuse my friend his apparently justified request.

Being dragged reluctantly into the fray, I was nominated by my comrades to stand as the National Front candidate in the Greenwich by-election in February 1987. It was a particularly violent campaign in which our members were constantly fighting with members of a new militant Marxist group called Anti-Fascist Action. I remember one particular incident in which I and a handful of colleagues were ambushed by a large group of Marxists. We were attacked and I felt sickened at my own cowardice in running from the scene. I looked back to see a friend of mine, a slightly-built man from Northern Ireland, fighting courageously against hopeless odds. He was half my size but had twice my courage. I realized that my heart was no longer in the war in which I was fighting and that my heartlessness had turned me into a coward. I felt guilty at my own cowardice, but also guilty that I had deserted my friend in the midst of the fight, leaving him to stand alone.

An hour or so later, the same mob of Marxists demanded the right to attend the National Front election meeting being held in a local school hall. I told the police that their only intent was to disrupt the meeting and that their presence was bound to lead to violence. The police insisted that they had a right to attend. As the Marxists took their seats in the hall, in close proximity to our own members, it was clear that the room had become a human time bomb, set to explode at any moment. As I rose to give my talk, I was heckled by the Marxists in the crowd. It was only a matter of time. Suddenly, blows were exchanged and the whole place erupted in a frenzy of punching, kicking, and chair-throwing. It's hard to describe the sheer noise and explosive mayhem of a riot inside a building. Most riots happen outside so that the anger, hatred, noise, and violence are dissipated by the openness of the space. In a confined space everything seems claustrophobically close, deafeningly loud, and excruciatingly intense. I resolved to make amends for my earlier act of cowardice by making a beeline for the largest Marxist I could see. In the midst of the madness I threw myself into the human hate-explosion and launched myself at the large Marxist, raining blow upon blow upon him. Within seconds it was over. The Marxists fled the building. We cleared up the mess, rearranged the chairs into tidy rows, and reconvened the meeting. My talk became a rabble-rousing war cry against our defeated enemies, my adrenaline buzzing through my body in triumphal bliss. There was no sign of the healing serenity of the preceding summer in the hateful frenzy of my rhetoric. The pagan warrior was once more in the ascendant, vanquishing the Christian penitent.

The pagan and the Christian could not coexist. Of necessity, one must survive at the expense of the other. For a short while it seemed that the pagan within me was resurrected. It fought for supremacy of my soul. The Christian lay dormant, seemingly dead. For a few sordid months I followed the pagan into the gutter, squirming in the squalor of the sewers into which it led me. I drank more than ever, seeking the silence of oblivion. I had my head shaved in a squalid pub in Leeds, an act of nihilistic hedonism. I recall a drunken debauch in Edinburgh in which I became increasingly miserable with every pint I drank. Incongruously I staggered from the pub to the Catholic cathedral for the vigil Mass. I was drunk and can only imagine what those who had the misfortune to be sitting next to me must have thought of the beer-breathed down-and-out in their midst. In my blurred memory of this pathetic episode, I felt like an outsider who wanted desperately to be inside. I was in the gutter but I was looking at the stars. I was lost at sea and in danger of perishing on life's surge but, deep down, I knew that I was in more need than ever of the ocean star, the guide who could save me from peril and from woe.

> Hail, Queen of heav'n, the ocean star,
> Guide of the wand'rer here below;
> Thrown on life's surge, we claim thy care:
> Save us from peril and from woe.
> Mother of Christ, star of the sea,
> Pray for the wand'rer, pray for me.

CHAPTER 20

COMING HOME

DURING THOSE dark months of 1987, locked in the dungeon of my own despair, I played the role of the political soldier with ever decreasing conviction, parroting slogans which I knew by heart but which my heart knew were false.

My rhetoric was empty. It was all bombast without fire. I had to escape.

Eventually, prompted by a personal relationship that had turned sour, I extracted myself from politics and found a job working for a printing company in the City of London. It was my first regular job in the wider world beyond the Party. I worked all day and drank most evenings. Every Friday afternoon I left work and walked to Liverpool Street station from whence I caught a train to Norwich in Norfolk, about 110 miles north-east of London. From Norwich I caught a taxi to Bungay, a small market town in Suffolk, where my children were now living. I spent all day on Saturday with the children and all night in the pubs. Like Chaucer's Friar I knew every tavern in the town, and every frequenter of the taverns knew me. I was finally building a network of friends who had no connection with politics. Thus, in a purely secular sense, life was beginning anew.

On Sunday mornings I took the children to Mass at the small Catholic church in the center of town. The parish priest was Father Richard Yeo, a gentle-spirited Benedictine who would later become abbot of Downside. Once again I found my soul soothed by the liturgy, bathing in the incense that filled the church and drinking deep draughts of wisdom from the Scriptures, from the prayers of the Mass, and from the homilies of the priest. My life was thus interwoven between the deep draughts of wisdom imbibed on Sundays and the even deeper draughts of ale imbibed throughout the remainder of the week. These two very distinct worlds formed the whole of my life, except for the forty hours each week that I was constrained by necessity to earn my daily bread.

Except for the hangover that occasionally gate-crashed my enjoyment of the liturgy on Sunday mornings, it might have been expected that the two worlds would never meet. One Saturday night, however, the twain not only met but collided. I had been drinking all night with a group of friends in Bungay and was expecting, as usual, to sleep in one of their houses at the night's end. As the night got more blurred, I became separated from my friends and realized at closing time that I was homeless. It was a cold night and in desperation I knocked on the door of the rectory. Father Yeo, whom I'd woken, led me to the guest room as I stammered and slurred my excuses and apologies. In the morning, bleary-eyed and hungover, I endured a silent breakfast of tea and toast with the priest. Once again, I stammered my apologies, stating penitentially that my drunken state the previous night was "pathetic." The priest said nothing. In my sullen pride, I recall feeling a little resentful that he didn't offer any words of comfort. In hindsight, I realized that his silence spoke more wisely than any platitudinous blandishments could have done.

Years later, in late 2000, I visited Downside Abbey to interview Dom Philip Jebb, Hilaire Belloc's grandson, as part of my research for my biography of his grandfather. During my brief stay at the monastery, I enjoyed a convivial meeting with Father Yeo, who was then the abbot. We reminisced fondly of our time in Bungay, both agreeing that we had left part of our heart in that charming Suffolk town, and he seemed genuinely astonished that I had not only become a Catholic but had written books, such as *Literary Converts* and my biography of Chesterton, of which he was clearly familiar. As with the earlier and less convivial meeting on the morning after my "pathetic" debauch, I found myself a little surprised that he was so surprised, and even a little irritated that he should think so little of my former self. Once again, however, I realize that he was right in his appraisal of me and that my annoyance was merely the pain of my own pride pricking my self-righteous ego. I was truly pathetic in those days and there could have been no inkling in the eyes of anyone who knew me that I was capable of anything worthwhile. God can indeed mould the most unpromising of clay.

Chastened by my intoxicated encounter with Fr. Yeo and other drunken excesses, I began to fear that I was dangerously dependent on alcohol. I knew that I wasn't physically addicted, in the normal sense in which an alcoholic is said to be addicted. I knew that I didn't suffer delirium tremens or other physical side effects if I abstained from alcohol. In prison, during the enforced abstinence from all alcoholic beverages, I never felt any effects beyond the natural (and healthy) desire to have a pint or two with friends. My concern was not that I was *physically* addicted but that I might be *emotionally* addicted. I wondered whether I was capable of abstaining from alcohol voluntarily. If I wasn't capable, I had a serious problem that needed addressing. It was with this concern in mind that I decided, in 1988, to give up all alcoholic beverages for Lent. I still went to the pub on weekends but I drank alcohol-free beer, instead of the microbrewed ale which was my normal beverage of choice. I can't say that I enjoyed it. The fake beer tasted so foul that I decided in subsequent years to simply drink fruit juice during Lent.

My decision to give up all booze for Lent was greeted with incredulity by my friends, none of whom thought for an instant that I would hold out for the whole six weeks. In truth, I'm not sure that I believed that I would be able to do so either. In the event, and as challenging as it was, I held out. I still remember going straight to the Horse and Groom from the Easter Sunday liturgy in Bungay in early April 1988 and ordering my first pint of real ale. How wonderful it tasted!

I have given up alcohol every Lent since then, finding it easier with each year that passes. These days I also give up tea and coffee, a much more challenging penance because, although I'm not physically addicted to alcohol, I *am* physically addicted to caffeine! Each year the first few days of Lent are spent in "cold turkey," suffering the fuzzy-headedness that goes with caffeine withdrawal.

As I was spending almost every weekend in Suffolk, returning to London on Sunday evenings, I decided to take the plunge and move to Norwich. I was, in any case, tired of London, a city which was tied up with the past from which I was trying to escape. I have no sympathy in this respect for Samuel Johnson's quip that "when a man is tired of London, he is tired of life." I grew tired of London because I had a zest for a life fuller than London could offer, a life in harmony with the permanent things which London's artificiality stifles. Thus, in April 1988, I shook the urban dust from my feet and returned to the beloved Shire of my childhood.

It has to be confessed and conceded that, strictly speaking, Norwich is in Norfolk, whereas the Shire of my childhood was Suffolk, which borders Norfolk to the south. In reality, however, the Shire of the South Folk (Suffolk) and the Shire of the North Folk (Norfolk) have more in common with each other than either county has with the rest of England. In my mind, Norfolk and Suffolk are unified in essentials. Their differences are merely accidental, philosophically speaking. For me, at least, they are essentially synonymous, the one blending seamlessly into the other.

The move to Norwich gave me a new lease of life. I enjoyed the charm of this historic city, with its mediaeval walls, castle, and cathedral, but I enjoyed even more the beauty of the surrounding countryside. Every Saturday I would cycle the fifteen miles to Bungay to see my children, normally returning the same day, and on Sunday I would set forth on my bike to explore the country lanes and villages of Norfolk. The most important discovery that I made at this time was the shrine of Our Lady of Walsingham, about thirty miles to the west of Norwich, which I would visit and revisit, week after week, especially during the summer months when pilgrims from all parts of England descended on this quaint and quiet corner of Norfolk. I would arrive for midday Mass and spend a few hours at the shrine and in the nearby village before returning home.

Walsingham had been one of the most important shrines of Christendom during the Middle Ages. Kings and paupers alike made the pilgrimage to this blessed spot at which, in 1061, the Lady of the Manor had seen an apparition of the Blessed Virgin. As I removed my shoes, as tradition dictates, to walk the Holy Mile barefoot from the Slipper Chapel to the village of Little Walsingham, as so many other Englishmen had done over the centuries, I found myself in communion with the Catholic England to which I now owed my allegiance. I was at one with England's saints and martyrs and at war with the secular spirit which put the English Martyrs to death.

Another positive consequence of my discovery of the shrine at Walsingham was the healing of the ingrained prejudice against the Blessed Virgin with which I had been afflicted for the whole of my life. I say "afflicted" but it might be as true to say that such prejudice is *inflicted* on the collective psyche of the English people by what

Belloc called the "ignorant wickedness" of "tom-fool Protestant history."* As I grew closer in prayer to Our Lady of Walsingham I was healed of the mistrust of Marian devotion, which is misnamed as Mariolatry by the Protestant propagandists. Such healing had begun with my sympathy for Chesterton's and Belloc's great love for the Mother of God and continued with the episode of the rosary in prison and the experience of Marian devotion at Our Lady Star of the Sea in Lowestoft. As I moved closer to Mary, accepting her as my Queen as I now accepted Christ as my King, I was simultaneously moving closer to the Catholic Church.

At around this time I developed the habit of trying to live my life in accordance with a "healthy trinity" of spiritual, physical, and intellectual exercise. Every day I sought to set aside adequate time for prayer, for physical exercise, and for serious intellectual or edifying reading. Even to this day, I keep the "healthy trinity" in mind as a means of ordering my daily routine.

Sometime during 1988 I began going to daily Mass, approaching the altar for a blessing and feeling a great hunger and desire for the Sacrament. I began instruction initially with Father Yeo in Bungay but subsequently with Monsignor Eugene Harkness at St. George's Parish in Norwich. At long last, on St. Joseph's Day 1989, I was received into the Catholic Church at Our Lady Mother of

---

* Hilaire Belloc to Hoffman Nickeerson, 13 September 1923; Belloc Collection, Boston College. Quoted in Joseph Pearce, *Old Thunder: A Life of Hilaire Belloc*, San Francisco: Ignatius Press, 2002, p. 230

God church on the outskirts of Norwich. My mother and father were in attendance and I rejoiced at their own happiness at my reception. My father was himself on the road to Rome, though I don't think he knew it at the time. He would be received into the Church several years later, a conversion which, to my mind, is perhaps even more miraculous than my own. I recall many discussions, heated at first, less so later, as we hammered out the meaning of the Faith. I remember reading Karl Adam's *Spirit of Catholicism* in the kitchen of my parents' home and discussing it with my father. The whole understanding of the Church as the Mystical Body of Christ and the Bride of Christ, one flesh in the primal Marriage that gives all marriage its meaning, had a huge impact on me and, I think, on my father also. We came to see that the Church is infallible because Christ is infallible.

On his deathbed in 2005, fortified by the sacraments of the Church, my father prayed the rosary with me and my wife as he prepared to cross the threshold of the Home that is every true "bead rattler's" reward. I hope and pray, and firmly believe, that flights of angels have sung him to his rest.

After the Mass at which I was received into the Church, and unbeknownst to me, a special reception had been organized. The ladies of the parish had baked a cake which, if my memory serves me correctly, had the words "Welcome Home Joe" emblazoned across it. I was asked to make a speech and found myself, for the first time in my life (and perhaps the last!), entirely lost for words. I had given many speeches in my time and was a master of impromptu rhetorical flourishes during my revolutionary days. But here I was, on the happiest and most important day of my life, completely and utterly tongue-tied. In truth, the sheer enormity of the occasion overwhelmed me. What could one say about something so miraculous, wondrous, salvific, terrific? There was nothing one could say, and perhaps nothing one should say. It was too large for words. And yet, put on the spot, I had to say something, however inadequate. All that I could say was that I had nothing to say—except that I had come home.

I had come home. Those four words say it all.

Hilaire Belloc, ironically a cradle Catholic and not a convert, has expressed the feeling of homecoming that accompanies every true conversion much better than I am able. In the absence of any adequate words of my own, I shall pass the microphone to him:

> The Faith, the Catholic Church, is discovered, is recognized, triumphantly enters reality like a landfall at sea which at first was thought a cloud. The nearer it is seen, the more is it real, the less imaginary: the more direct and external its voice, the more indubitable its representative character, its "persona," its voice. The metaphor is not that men fall in love with it: the metaphor is that they discover home. 'This was what I sought. This was my need.' It is the very mould of the mind, the matrix to which corresponds in every outline the outcast and unprotected contours of the soul. It is Verlaine's "Oh! Rome—oh! Mere!" And

that not only to those who had it in childhood and have returned, but much more—and what a proof! —to those who come upon it from over the hills of life and say to themselves "Here is the town."*

---

* Hilaire Belloc to E. S. P. Haynes, November 8, 1923; quoted in Robert Speaight, *The Life of Hilaire Belloc*, Freeport, New York: Books for Libraries Press, 1970, p. 377.

CHAPTER 21

LOVE AND REASON

ON THE mundane surface, nothing much seemed to have changed after my reception into the Church. I still had the same nine-to-five job at a book wholesaler, which I had taken upon my move to Norwich, and I'm sure that my friends and work colleagues would not have noticed any miraculous change. I had certainly not become a saint overnight, nor would I become a saint after a thousand and one more nights! I am, however, making progress. My soul, like the soul of every one of life's pilgrims, is a work in progress. Evidence of any change could only be seen by looking back across the months and years. Although I had grown significantly, my spiritual growth was as imperceptible on a daily basis as is the physical growth of a child. I was aware, however, that my reception into the Catholic Church was absolutely necessary to my continued progress. My first confession had cleansed me of my sins, enabling me to move forward with a clean slate, and my regular reception of the Blessed Sacrament supplied the very bread of my life, nourishing me with grace and enabling me to grow healthier.

Although my first confession had cleansed me of my numerous past sins, it did not remove the responsibility that I had to make amends for all the damage that my sins had caused. My life since my conversion has, therefore, been an ongoing act of atonement. In particular, I have sought to use the gifts that God has given me to glorify Him and to bring souls to Him, in contrast to the way that I had previously used those same gifts to glorify his enemies and to lead souls astray. This has been the rationale behind my vocation as a Catholic writer in the twenty-five years since my conversion.

The first book that I wrote following my conversion was a life of Otto Strasser, the disillusioned Nazi and enemy of Hitler who had been so influential in helping me to take the first faltering steps in the direction of faith. Upon its completion, I faced the problem of trying to find a publisher. I knew that I could not disclose my real name, due to my notoriety as a racist, and decided that I would need a *nom de plume*. After giving it some thought I decided to write under the name of "Robert Williamson." The name had palpable significance because of the appearance of a "Bob Williamson" in a Loyalist song called "The Old Orange Flute." In the song, which I had learned during my days as a member of the Orange Order, Bob Williamson outrages his Protestant Loyalist brethren by becoming a Catholic. As a former member of the Orange Order who had become a Catholic, I saw myself as a reincarnation of the character in the song. Since the ghost of Bob Williamson would return to haunt me in a mystically symbolic way many years later and since, therefore, we will be returning to him, it would be helpful to give the opening lines of the song, which were the source and inspiration of my adoption of Bob Williamson's name:

In the County Tyrone,
Near the town of Dungannon,
Where many a ruction myself had a han' in,
Bob Williamson lived there,
A weaver by trade,
And all of us thought him
A stout Orange blade. . . .

But the cunning young coo boy
Sure took us all in
And married a Papish
Called Bridget McGinn;
Turned Papish himself
And forsook the old cause
That gave us our freedom
Religion and laws.

Now the boys of the town,
They made some noise upon it,
And Bob had to fly
To the province of Connaught;
Took with him his wife
And his fixin's, to boot,
And along with the rest
Went the Old Orange Flute.

Each Sunday at Mass,
To atone for past deeds,

Bob said Paters and Aves
And counted his beads. . . .

Although I was not from County Tyrone, and though I had not "married a papish," the parallels between my situation and that of Bob Williamson were nonetheless striking. It was extremely unusual for an Orangeman to convert to Catholicism, as unthinkable a faux pas in the sectarian North of Ireland as a member of the Ku Klux Klan marrying a black woman in the South of the United States. The unlikelihood of our situation and our parallel lives had transformed the legendary Orange renegade into my spiritual and inspirational doppelgänger. Bob Williamson and I were one and I adopted his name as a mark of respect as well as a convenient mask with which to hide my true identity.

I received several rejection letters for my biography of Strasser before a small publisher, based in east London, expressed an interest. At the publisher's request, I travelled to its tiny offices above a store in Brick Lane market, in Bethnal Green, a place that had been the scene of many fights between NF members and our rivals in the Socialist Workers Party. Considering Brick Lane's association with my dim and not so distant past, it felt odd to return there in such different circumstances. It felt decidedly odder when the publishers turned out to be a couple of militant Zionist Jews whose interest in the manuscript was obviously connected to its negative depiction of Hitler. I wondered what they would have thought of the former anti-Semite in their midst if they could see behind the disguise that Bob Williamson provided.

I was not particularly impressed by the damp-ridden premises in which the two men did business and was decidedly less impressed with the hostelry to which they took me to discuss the prospects of their publishing my book. The latter was a sordid pub in Whitechapel at which a stripper was disrobing to the accompaniment of loud and awful music. The surreal irony of the whole situation was accentuated by the fact that I was going direct from my meeting with the seedy publishers to my first pilgrimage to Rome. Imagine the sheer surreal weirdness of the scene: a former neo-Nazi and recent convert to Catholicism, en route to Rome, in conference with two seedy Zionist Jews to the accompaniment of a striptease artist! The black comedy continued when I politely refused to give any money to the stripper, as she came round collecting tips, on the basis that I had made a deliberate point of averting my eyes from her performance. I think she was more offended by the averting of my gaze than by the refusal of the tip! I bid goodbye to my potential collaborators, appreciating the grim humor of the scenario in which I had just found myself but also feeling decidedly grimy from the whole experience. Oh, how splendidly sane was the Eternal City after this brief sojourn in Gomorrah.

In shaking the dust from my shoes with regard to the seedy publisher, I was thereby condemning the manuscript of the Otto Strasser biography to gather dust indefinitely. It has never been published and is now nestling in someone's attic somewhere in England, almost lost and nearly forgotten. *Sic transit Gloria mundi.*

Undeterred by the faltering fortunes of the Strasser book, I embarked immediately on the writing of my biography of G. K. Chesterton. I was motivated in part by my dissatisfaction with the existing biographies of him and partly by a desire to disseminate the astonishing wisdom of the writer who, under grace, was more responsible than anyone in bringing me to Christ. I see the writing of this book as a two-fold act of thanksgiving. It was an act of thanksgiving to God for leading me to Chesterton but also an act of thanksgiving to Chesterton for leading me to God.

I was convinced as I wrote the book that Chesterton and those other great thinkers who led me to faith had done so exclusively through the power of reason. I remained convinced for many years that my conversion was a purely rational process. It was the triumph of sense over nonsense; the affirmation of the inextricable bond between *fides et ratio*. I would have argued vehemently and vociferously against any suggestion that my conversion had an emotional component. I now understand, however, that a process of healing coincided with the engagement with reason, a healing process that was not contrary to reason but was necessary to it.

Although one can argue rationally from a purely philosophical understanding of transcendentals, such as goodness, truth, and beauty, to the existence of a transcendental God, it is much more difficult to argue rationally against our own prejudices. Hatred and bigotry, both of which are the bitter fruits of pride, are self-encapsulating prisons, locking the intellect within the constraining confines of the self-centered ego. There is no way out of this prison of pride without the key provided by God-given grace. It is this grace which provides the supernatural healing power that allows us to desire a truth beyond the self and its self-referential constraints. Without this key there is no escape from the debilitating and Gollumizing tendency of pride. In short, and to put the matter bluntly, without the healing power of grace we are not be able to reason our way to God because we will lack the desire to engage with the reality beyond ourselves. In refusing this grace, we excommunicate ourselves from the world of objective reality, exorcising the power of reason instead of exercising it. In so doing, we condemn ourselves to life imprisonment, turning our very lives into a living death sentence.

Since this necessary grace is the manifestation of God's love, it can be seen that the power of love as well as the power of reason is needed for the conversion of every heart and mind. The power that heals the pride in our hearts is the love that we receive directly from God's Sacred Heart but also the love of His that we receive from the hearts of others who truly love us. It is for this reason that I benefited in a priceless way from the love I received from relative strangers and even enemies, such as the policemen who lent me money, the punk who invited me to the pub, and the Jewish member of the National Council for Civil Liberties who laid down his living, if not strictly speaking his life, to defend my freedom.

At this juncture, it is important to stress that true love, like anything else that is true, is truly rational. It accords with reason. There is nothing irrational about love, truly conceived and truly practiced. It is important—indeed crucial and necessary—to distinguish between the rational love, practiced and preached by true Christians, and the irrational "love," practiced and preached by the world. There is a gaping chasm between the one and the other. John Lennon and Jesus Christ do not mean the same thing by "love." For Lennon and his ilk love is first and foremost a feeling, something irrational and purely subjective. It is about "doing our own thing" and "marching to the beat of our own drum." It is essentially self-centered. It is the erotic manifestation of the creed of Polonius, which had exerted such a disastrous influence on my own life: "This above all: To thine own self be true." It is a love that sacrifices the lover on the altar of self-worship and self-gratification. The love that is happy to break hearts and kill babies. It is, like all other manifestations of pride, an act of self-deification.

In contrast to this false worldly love, true love is inseparable from self-sacrifice. It is the laying down of our lives for the beloved. As with reason, it leads us out of ourselves and in pursuit of the Other. It is not a feeling but an act. Indeed, for the Christian, it is not simply an act but a commandment. The two great commandments of Christ are that we love the Lord our God and that we love our neighbor. They are commandments that must be obeyed even if—especially if—the love is not accompanied by any positive feelings. The policeman, punk rocker, and civil rights activist would not have felt anything good about me; on the contrary, each would have fought against natural feelings of aversion towards me. Their acts of love were all the more powerful precisely because no such feelings of attraction were present.

I now understand that love, as well as reason, was necessary for my conversion, but I understand also that the love to which I am indebted is as rational as the reason. As the Greek and the Christian philosophers could have told me, love and reason are inseparable because goodness and truth are inseparable. They are one because they have their source in the One. It is, therefore, clear to me now that I was as attracted as much by Chesterton's goodness as I was by the truth that he espoused. He was a man alive to love as he was a man alive to truth. In everything he wrote, the virtue and the verity were one and indivisible. He thought clearly and loved truly.

I am also aware now that I was as attracted as much by the goodness of Chesterton's humor as by the goodness of his heart. His humor and humility found expression in an irrepressible and irresistible *joie de vivre*, a love of life that was the apogee and epitome of the laughter and the love of friends of which his friend Hilaire Belloc wrote. For Chesterton, God was not only the Good, the True, and the Beautiful but also the good-humored King who gave the gift of laughter to Man. We reason because God is Reason; we love because God is Love; we create because God creates—and we laugh because God laughs.

These are all marks of the Divine Image in Man. The other creatures do not reason, love, create, or laugh. Humor is human because it is divine. Thus in *The Man Who was Thursday* Chesterton wrote of the humor of God to be found in nature, describing the absurd appearance of the hornbill, "which was simply a huge yellow beak with a small bird tied on behind it." Syme, the novel's protagonist, had the sensation upon seeing this odd and eccentric bird that "Nature was always making quite mysterious jokes. . . . He wondered whether even the archangels understood the hornbill."* In *Orthodoxy*, Chesterton wrote that there "was some one thing that was too great for God to show us when He walked upon our earth; and I have sometimes fancied that it was His mirth."† He also wrote in the same masterful volume that "the laughter of the heavens is too loud for us to hear."‡ Even death, from the perspective of the Resurrected, is very much a laughing matter. Hence, in Chesterton's poem "The Skeleton," the skull's unchanging grin, or its "chuckle spread from ear to ear" as Eliot put it in *The Waste Land*, is a reflection of the divine sense of humor:

> Chattering finch and water-fly
> Are not merrier than I;
> Here among the flowers I lie
> Laughing everlastingly.
> No: I may not tell the best:
> Surely, friends, I might have guessed
> Death was but the good King's jest,
> It was hid so carefully.

---

* G. K. Chesterton, *The Man Who was Thursday*, London: Penguin Books, 1986, p. 160

† G. K. Chesterton, *Orthodoxy*, London: John Lane Company, 1908, 168

‡ Ibid., p. 167

If this somewhat lengthy Chestertonian digression seems a little out of place in the closing pages of this account of my own journey to faith, I can only apologize by stating that Chesterton is present at the end of my journey because he has been ever-present since its beginning. I have returned to Chesterton at the last because he has continually returned to me as the paradoxical first and last, repeatedly reorienting me towards the good, the true, the beautiful, and the divinely comic.

I will end my journey with a strange tale which offers a fleeting glimpse of the Divine Comedy of which Chesterton speaks.

In the summer of 1999, after I had been a Catholic for a little over ten years, I was asked to be the resident tutor at a summer program organized by the Phoenix Institute at Brasenose College, Oxford. One of the students was a beautiful American lady who was destined, less than two years later, to become my wife. Little did I know when we first met that she would unwittingly be the means by which the ghost of Bob Williamson would be resurrected. It will be recalled that I considered this Orangeman who became a Catholic to be my spiritual doppelgänger. The difference was that, unlike Bob Williamson, I was not "from the County Tyrone, near the town of Dungannon," nor had I "married a papish called Bridget McGinn." Imagine my surprise when I discovered that my wife, who was from California, a very long way from Tyrone, *was* the daughter of a woman "from the County Tyrone, near the town of Dungannon." My mother-in-law had been born and raised in a small village in Tyrone called The Rock before emigrating to England and eventually to the United States. To my astonishment, I realized that I had not "married a papish called Bridget McGinn" but that I had married her daughter! The odds against such a coincidence are too astronomical to be the work of blind chance. God does indeed make "quite mysterious jokes," as Chesterton claimed, but perhaps, on the rare occasions when his good humor is evident, the laughter of the heavens is not quite too loud for us to hear.

Although it seems decorous to end the journey with an affirmation of love and reason, it also seems appropriate to conclude with the observation that the journey from racial hatred to rational love is a comedy in the true sense in which it has a happy ending. And yet, of course, and lest I be seen as indulging in premature triumphalism, the journey is not yet over. Life is a perilous quest and I am still very much on it. I have my dragons to face and my sins to be forgiven. I have not yet reached the happy ending but I have at least seen glimpses of the glories it promises. The ultimate happy ending which every rational soul desires, and for which my own soul fervently prays, is the fullness of communion, forever and ever, with the Love that moves the sun and all the stars.*

---

* I could think of no better way of ending my own journey towards the Divine than with this translation of the final climactic line of Dante's *Paradiso*.

POSTSCRIPT

NEW LIFE, NEW WORLD

INSOFAR AS my reception into the Catholic Church was a homecoming, it was also a consummation. It was the culmination of the journey from racial hatred to rational love. It was the end of my life, in the sense that it was the fulfillment of its end, its purpose. And yet, at the same time, it was also the beginning of a new life in communion with Christ in His Church. Life had indeed begun anew. My sins forgiven. The slate wiped clean. The new life was not, however, a negation of the old life but its fulfillment. My sinful life and the lessons it taught had led me to the foot of the Cross. My path was that of Mary Magdalen. She and I were miserable sinners, forgiven by Christ and invited by Him to become His disciples. In this sense we should not regret the path that we have taken, however wayward, if it had eventually led us Home. I am reminded of an interview that Malcolm Muggeridge gave shortly after he had been received into the Catholic Church at the ripe old age of seventy-nine. Asked whether he had regretted the pleasure that his sins, especially his adulterous affairs, had given him, he replied that he regretted the harm and the suffering that his sins had caused (alluding primarily, no doubt, to his long-suffering wife) but that he could not regret his life, taken in its totality, because it had led him to Christ and His Church.

Although my reception into the Church was the end of the journey from racial hatred to rational love, it was not the end of my life's journey. I am still a miserable sinner and the race with the devil is anything but over. In an effort to stay one step ahead of him, I continue to practice the healthy trinity of spiritual, physical, and intellectual exercise, endeavoring to strike the right balance between the life of prayer, the life of the body, and the life of the mind. Regarding the first of these, the sacramental life of the Church is at the very heart of my own life. Receiving the Blessed Sacrament at Mass provides the spiritual nourishment for the journey; receiving God's forgiveness in the Sacrament of Penance helps me to grow in virtue and begin anew whenever I stumble and fall into sin; and every day my wife and I pray to our "Blessed Immaculate Mother for all the graces available to us today through the Sacrament of Matrimony." Without God's love, poured forth in sacramental grace, and without my willing cooperation with it, I would lose my race with the devil and lose my eternal life with Christ into the bargain.

As I embarked on my new life as a Catholic, I was aware that I had a long way to go. The remnants of the old man, the pre-conversion "me," clung on tenaciously to the new man I was trying to become, dogging my steps. Looking back over the years, with the wisdom that only hindsight can attain, I can see how the old man has faded and the new man has grown, *Deo gratias et laus Deo*, which is not to say that much more growth is still needed and desired!

A large part of my early years as a Catholic was spent on the researching and writing of my biography of Chesterton. I worked on the book from 1991 until 1995, in the tiny studio apartment in Norwich in which I lived, after returning home from my regular job. Most weekday evenings, from around 6:30pm until around midnight, I would work diligently on this labor of love, immersing myself in all things Chestertonian. After I had finished it, I prayed fervently that I would secure a good publisher, the bitter memory of my disappointment with regard to the earlier biography of Strasser fresh in my mind. My earnest hope, which I articulated in my prayers, was that the book would go some way in repairing the damage that my former life had caused. Whereas my previous writing had led people astray, I hoped that my gifts as a writer could now help to lead people to the truth. I recall a conversation with my father in the Crooked Billet, a pub near my parents' home, in which I told him that I would be content to die if the Chesterton biography were published, happy in the knowledge that I had at least achieved something worthwhile in my life. As I look back on those prayers and that conversation, I am astounded and astonished anew at how generous God has been in the years that followed. Not only did a major secular publisher, Hodder and Stoughton, accept the manuscript for publication but in the following years an even larger publisher, HarperCollins, would publish several more of my books. Such a scenario would have been beyond my wildest dreams in 1995.

The Chesterton biography was published in the summer of 1996. A few weeks later, the *Daily Telegraph* published an article with the headline, "Chesterton Author's National Front Past." I had a pretty good idea that the person who had informed the *Telegraph* of my identity was an embittered former political comrade of mine, intent on avenging my opposition to him in one of the National Front's interminable internecine feuds. I was not shocked to see the article. In fact, I was expecting it. I had decided to submit the manuscript to the publisher under my real name and not under the *nom de plume*, "Robert Williamson," knowing the likelihood—indeed the inevitability—of the connection with my past being discovered. My rationale for doing so was simple. It seemed to me that there were only two things one could do with the skeleton in one's closet. One could lock it away and hide the key, living in fear that the key and the skeleton will one day be discovered, or one could leave the closet door carelessly unlocked, indeed slightly and conspicuously ajar, in the hope and expectation that it will be discovered. The discovery, however unpleasant at the time, would be a liberation from fear and from the necessity of living a lie.

Having received the contract and the advance from Hodder and Stoughton, I perceived that I had come to a crossroads in my life. I knew that I could never write another book under the same grueling conditions, working in a nine-to-five job during the day and researching and writing a book in the evenings. The four years of almost obsessive labor on the Chesterton book could not and would not be repeated. The enormity of the commitment was too much. It was a marathon that I did not have the stamina to repeat. I was, therefore, faced with a simple choice. I could rest on my laurels, content that my prayers had been answered and my dreams had come true in the publication of my book by a major publisher, or else I could give up my nine-to-five job and take the plunge as a fulltime writer. The latter option would involve a leap of faith that some might have considered reckless because I had no savings or other assets and would need to survive on the money I had received from the publisher, hoping that I could write another book and receive another advance before the money ran out. Reckless or not, I chose the latter option and became a fulltime writer in April 1996. Over the next five years, until September 2001, I earned a living of sorts as a writer, becoming the stereotypical struggling author doomed to garret poverty. I was helped by the generosity of a good friend, Alf Simmonds, who served as an occasional benefactor in times of financial crisis, for which I shall always be grateful.

The first thing that I did as a fulltime writer was to exorcise from myself the ghost of a novel that had been haunting me for some time. It was not a good novel, if indeed it can be called a novel at all, and in some ways I regret that it was ever published. My only reason for mentioning it is that the writing of it coincided with, and was perhaps the cause of, a curious mystical experience. On a beautiful sunny day, an all too rare occurrence in England, I decided to spend the morning on a bench in a nearby cemetery, writing the novel in a notebook. I spent a fruitful few hours basking in the sun, communing with my pen and waxing lyrical about the mysterious relationship between time and eternity which was an essential ingredient of my embryonic work of fiction. Feeling that I needed a break, I decided to say the rosary before heading to a local bakery for lunch. I looked at my watch, noticed that it was 12:15 and then laid down in the grass between the tombstones to tell my beads. My morning's musings on the nature of time and eternity seemed to elevate the contemplative aspect of my prayer, enabling me to enter into the rosary's mysteries in a manner that my too easily distracted mind rarely accomplishes. It would not be an exaggeration to describe my prayer on this occasion as a mystical experience, transporting me out of myself into a contemplation of the timeless.

Having finished the rosary, I put the beads back in my pocket and looked at my watch. It was 12:15. I looked again. It was definitely 12:15, the same time that it had been when I had begun my prayers. I thought that my watch must have stopped. I checked again. It hadn't. The only logical possibility was that I had misread the watch before starting my prayers. Yet this seemed an odd explanation, especially in the light of the mystical dimension of my prayerful meditations. I am, however, a natural skeptic and have always sympathized with John Henry Newman's quip that mysticism begins in mist and ends in schism. I find it hard to believe that I was literally transported out of time during my prayer, or that time stood still. Perhaps I did misread the watch. Whatever the explanation, natural or supernatural (or both), I considered the "time-stopping" experience a gift of God, a Divine blessing on my musing and meditation on the mystery of things. If the prosaic explanation for the "miracle" was my misreading of the watch, it was still a fortunate and mystically providential coincidence that I should misread it at such a time and under such mystically transcendent circumstances. In exorcising the ghost of the novel, I had raised the ghost of a mystery that has haunted me ever since.

Having written the novel, I embarked on the research for my book, *Literary Converts*, a much more challenging project. I spent several exhilarating and engrossing weeks in the late summer of 1996 scouring through hundreds of books in the literature section of the University of East Anglia library. I was enthralled to discover the way in which the Catholic Literary Revival constituted a network of minds energizing each other. In my research and during the subsequent writing of the book I had the joy of working with the *eminenti* of modern English literature: John Henry Newman, Gerard Manley Hopkins, Oscar Wilde, G. K. Chesterton, Siegfried Sassoon, Edith Sitwell, Maurice Baring, Ronald Knox, T. S. Eliot, Evelyn Waugh, Graham Greene, Roy Campbell, Muriel Spark, C. S. Lewis, and J. R. R. Tolkien.

At the beginning of 1997, *The Lord of the Rings* was voted the greatest book of the century in a nationwide poll. The response of the self-styled literati to Tolkien's triumph was an unhealthy and unholy mixture of ridicule and contempt: *The Lord of the Rings* was ridiculed and those who voted for it were treated with contempt. Provoked by the supercilious ignorance of the critics, most of whom had clearly never even read Tolkien's masterpiece before dismissing it, I decided to write a book about Tolkien's life and work, concentrating on Tolkien's lifelong Catholic faith and the ways in which, in the author's own judgment, *The Lord of the Rings* was "a fundamentally religious and Catholic work." The book was published by HarperCollins as *Tolkien: Man and Myth* in 1998. HarperCollins also published *Literary Converts*, though not until the following year.

It was whilst I was working on the Tolkien book that I wrote to Alexander Solzhenitsyn, requesting an interview with him. The subsequent visit to Russia, during which I had the inestimable honor of interviewing him in his home near Moscow, remains one of the greatest moments of my life. I am also gratified to know that the great Russian writer approved of my biography of him. Other books on which I worked at this time included *Flowers of Heaven: One Thousand Years of Christian Verse* and *Small is Still Beautiful*, an appraisal of the continuing relevance and importance of Schumacher's political and economic vision, which had been so influential on my own intellectual development. I wrote *The Unmasking of Oscar Wilde* as a corrective to the meretricious myths surrounding Wilde's life, especially the nonsense propagated by Richard Ellmann in his confused and confusing biography. Whereas Ellmann and others had drawn a picture of Wilde as a moral iconoclast and (homo) sexual liberator, I highlighted Wilde's lifelong love affair with the Catholic Church, which was consummated on his death bed by his conversion *in extremis*.

In 1999 I was invited by the Phoenix Institute to be the resident tutor for the final week of their annual summer program in Oxford. In need of the additional money, I readily accepted, taking up residence at Brasenose College in late July. I didn't know it but the following days were destined to change my life forever. Amongst the students was a young and beautiful American lady, whose smile and personality shone forth with an arresting brightness. Her name was Susannah Brown, a native of California who had recently received a Masters degree in theology from Franciscan University in Steubenville. After she returned to the States, a long distance relationship developed, slowly ascending in intimacy from e-mail, to instant messaging and then to phone conversations. At some point, imperceptibly, the friendship had matured into courtship. Feeling the need to take things to the next step, it was agreed that Susannah should visit me in England. I think we were both very nervous as the planned visit loomed ever closer. What if we realized upon meeting again in the flesh that we had nothing in common? What if we didn't even like each other? The prospect of being awkwardly polite to each other for ten days or so, counting down the days until the scheduled departure, was a dauntingly ominous prospect. Such fears evaporated within moments of our meeting at Heathrow airport. We got on splendidly, taking walks in the Norfolk countryside, saying the rosary together in the car as we drove to places of interest, and generally rejoicing in each other's company.

I was now living in Swaffham, a small market town about twenty-five miles to the west of Norwich. Susannah was staying in the local convent. Each morning we would meet in the convent chapel and each evening I would return her to the safekeeping of the sisters by the curfew hour of nine o'clock. It was midsummer, which, in England, means that it doesn't get dark until after 10pm. It was, therefore, ordained by a congruence of religious rule and astronomical law that we would have no romantic moonlit nights.

During Susannah's second visit, I proposed to her as we knelt before the Blessed Sacrament in the Slipper Chapel at Walsingham, a place that had always nurtured and nourished my faith. Although I quipped that I had chosen this particular scenario because we were both already on our knees and it saved me the embarrassment of having to kneel in front of her, in reality I wanted to offer myself to her in union with my offering of myself to Christ in the Blessed Sacrament and to Our Lady of Walsingham at the shrine dedicated to her. It was important that we began as we meant to go on, offering our love for each other in self-sacrificial witness to Christ and His Immaculate Mother.

In December 2000 I made my first ever visit to the United States to meet Susannah's parents at their home in Southern California. On St. Stephen's Day, or Boxing Day as it is known in England, the day after Christmas, I took a two mile walk along the river to a charming café on the beach, at which I basked in the sun, sipping fig milkshake. It was a far cry from the chilly Christmases back home!

I made my second visit to the States in April for our wedding. We were married at St. Peter's church in Steubenville, where Susannah was living, and honeymooned in Rome and in the beautiful Tuscan city of Lucca, birthplace of Puccini and resting place of the relics of Saints Rita and Gemma. In Rome we had our marriage blessed by John Paul II, Susannah looking beautiful and resplendent in her wedding dress. In early May we returned to my house in

Swaffham, my new wife having sold almost all of her possessions to begin a new life with me in England.

I realized that marriage would mean the end of my bohemian days as a fulltime writer. I had been living on royalties from my books, supplementing my income by working two nights a week at the local gym. It was clear, however, that a more stable and consistent source of income would be needed, especially with the prospect of children being added to the domestic equation. I was in the midst of writing my biography of Hilaire Belloc and resolved to get myself a regular job, of any sort, as soon as the book was finished. Imagine my surprise, therefore, when, a few weeks after our return from honeymoon, I received a phone call from Nick Healy, President of Ave Maria College in Michigan, which would later metamorphose into Ave Maria University in Florida, offering me a job as writer in residence at the new school. The phone call heralded a period of rapid and radical change for the newly-weds, turning our lives upside down. Scrambling to get all the necessary documents together to secure the visa, we moved to the United State on Friday, September 7, four days before the 9/11 attacks. In fact, my first day of classes at Ave Maria College was on 9/11 itself, making my arrival in the States something of a baptism of fire.

In the space of a few months my wife had sold almost all of her possessions to move to England and I had sold almost all of mine to move to the United States. We were, therefore, starting our new lives in the New World with nothing except our hopes for the future. I was now forty years old and it was no wonder that I found myself musing on the old adage that this was the age at which life begins. Actually I had never taken this particular aphorism particularly seriously. It was, I thought, somewhat preposterous to suggest that life began when it was, for most people, already more than half over. I was, however, forced to think again. Having adopted the rustic habits of a hobbit in the rural surroundings of the Shire in which I had made my home for the previous thirteen years, ever since my escape from London, the prospect of a new life in the New World filled me with a Frodo-like fear of the Unknown. And yet there was also the thrilling sense of adventure that accompanied my arrival in the United States, only four days before the forces of Mordor made their infamous and infernal attack upon the Two Towers. As I found myself in mysterious and uncharted cultural waters it felt as if I had sailed into the Mystic West.

Perhaps "Mystic Michigan" is not a juxtaposition that would present itself readily to most Americans, most of whom would see very little that is mystical about the midwest, but to an Englishman who had never previously lived abroad, my arrival in the United States had the unmistakable feel of an exciting new adventure. It was, indeed, a somewhat unsettling experience to realize that, in spite of the absence of a language barrier (well, almost!) in the United States, I felt more at home in Italy, a country I had visited often, than in America.

As if a new wife and a new life in the New World were not enough "adventure" for one year, the release of the film version of the first part of *The Lord of the Rings* added to the heady mixture of novelty. As the author of one book on Tolkien and the editor of another, I found myself cited as an "expert" on Middle-earth. All of a sudden I was being interviewed for television, for film documentaries, for newspapers, magazines, and on numerous radio talks shows. "Talking Tolkien" became almost a full-time occupation, squeezed somehow between my teaching commitments at Ave Maria College. I travelled to many parts of the United States and Canada giving talks on the Catholic dimension of *The Lord of the Rings*, speaking at Ivy League schools, such as Harvard, Princeton and Yale, at state universities, small liberal arts colleges, literary conferences, diocesan conferences, and at local parishes. Life during this period was both exhilarating and exhausting.

On St. Patrick's Day 2002 our son Leo was born. He has Down's syndrome and would later be diagnosed as having autism. What a joy he has been over the past eleven years! What a joy and what a blessing! Father Ho Lung of the Missionaries of the Poor, whose biography I have been blessed to write for Saint Benedict Press, describes those with Down's syndrome as "by definition, love": "They live on love, and they live to love. They are basic elemental human nature, in all its beauty and simplicity. We know that if anyone has a Down's syndrome child, they can be sure that joy, laughter, and love have been given to them as a special gift from God. . . . There is no ambition, no battle for power, no pomp, no falsehood, no hypocrisy in the Down's syndrome people."* As Leo's father, I know

---

* Joseph Pearce, Candles in the Dark: *The Authorized Biography of Father Richard Ho Lung and the Missionaries of the Poor*, Charlotte, NC: Saint Benedict Press, 2013, p. 115-117

from the beauty of experience that our son is a special gift from God. He has brought joy, laughter and love to our family, as well as challenges that are themselves gifts. It has been said that most of us are given life in order to learn whereas a special few are given life in order to teach. How true this is. Leo has taught us so much. He has taught us to love more truly. He has taught us to give ourselves more fully. He has helped us to lay down our lives for those we love. Could he have given us any greater gift? How wicked is a world that shuns such gifts! How wicked that children with Down's syndrome are hunted down in the womb and systematically exterminated. How wicked that a mother has the "right" to choose to kill her own unborn children. How wicked that mothers are encouraged to kill their own "imperfect" babies, discriminating against the weak, the infirm and the disabled.

When Leo was only a few days old it was discovered that he had a hole in his heart that would require surgery when he was about two-years-old. Susannah and I decided to pray a rosary novena to St. Philip Neri requesting his intercession that Leo's heart might be healed without surgery. For nine consecutive months we prayed this rosary and we considered it significant that Leo's next appointment was scheduled for the day after the nine months of prayers were completed. We went to the appointment confident that our prayers had been answered. The cardiologist listened to Leo's heart with his stethoscope and informed us that the heart murmur indicated that the hole was still there. His diagnosis confirmed the medical student's diagnosis immediately before. Therefore, two independent assessments seemed to show that our prayers for healing had not been answered. Undeterred, Susannah requested an echocardiogram. The cardiologist looked surprised, and a little irritated that we should question his diagnosis. Nonetheless, Leo was given the sonogram and the doctor was somewhat mortified and no doubt embarrassed that he had been proven wrong. There was no hole in the heart! Ever since then, St. Philip Neri has been a special favorite.

Tragedy struck our family at the end of 2004 when the little girl in Susannah's womb died. She was eight months old *in utero*. I cradled the cute little lifeless girl in my arms, tears trickling down my face, and looked up at the crucifix over our bed. For the first and only time in my life, I felt myself nailed to the Cross with Our Lord instead of nailing him there with my sins. It was as if Christ had reached down and lifted me up onto His Cross, sharing it with me and making me one with Him. I cannot explain the deep sense of consoling peace that this mystical moment bestowed. We named our little daughter Giavanna Paolina, or Gianna for short, in honor of John Paul II and St. Gianna Molla, and laid her to rest in a tiny white coffin in the Garden of Innocence, the children's section of the cemetery, which was filled with tiny coffins like hers. May flights of angels sing her and the other little ones to their rest.

Words are clearly inadequate to describe the tragedy and trauma of losing a child but I did my best to convey the agony and the passion, and the hope and the resurrection, in a sonnet entitled "First Decade," which I wrote for Susannah on the occasion of our tenth wedding anniversary in 2011:

On Walsingham's wings Love alights,
Announcing at Our Lady's shrine
His blessing on the troth He plights
That makes thee mine, and makes me thine.

Agony's garden crowns with thorn,
In passion's sweat and labour's pain,
The child of ours to His arms born,
Burying death with grace's grain.

In easter'd splendour from the tomb
He rises from the death that died,
Blesses the unborn in your womb,
The scars of loss, the eyes that cried.

And so, my love, His love is thine,
And, through His love, I know thee mine.

There was more heartbreak as Susannah suffered two miscarriages and was then diagnosed with endometriosis. Surgery was needed to remove one of her ovaries. We were now both in our forties and it began to look as though we would not be blessed with any more children. We continued to pray doggedly but not very hopefully until, out of the blue and against all expectation, Susannah fell pregnant once again. On leap day 2008 another little girl was born. We named her Evangeline Marie, in honor of the Blessed Virgin but also because she was "good news." Indeed, she was not merely good news but the best possible news imaginable!

And that brings the story pretty much up to date. I write this in my office, seated by a window overlooking Ladydale, the name we've given to the little piece of land we own. As the wood in which I used to play as a child had been named Ladywood by my ancestors in honor of Our Lady, so the valley in which I play with my own children is named Ladydale in her honor also. And so the Faith that gave birth to the Old World is resurrected in the New.

Through the window I see the chicken coop that Susannah and I built during this past Lent and into which we moved our chickens on Holy Saturday. It feels good to be finally practicing in a small but beautiful way the distributism that Belloc, Chesterton, and Schumacher preached. It feels good to hear our own rooster crowing in the morning, the herald of each new dawn.

The crowing of the cock is, of course, not merely a clarion call but also a symbol of the betrayal of Christ by his disciples. It serves, therefore, as a painful reminder of my weaknesses and failings, and my tendency to fall with monotonous regularity. No, my race with the devil is not won but it is consoling to know that the final victory is not his. The victory is with the Rising of the Son:

> *Corpus Christi!*
> Rising through the rose,
> *Sanguis Christi!*
> Skyward flows.
> Heavenly Host
> So new, so old,

As Holy Ghost
Turns snow to gold.
Joy to Glory,
Tinged with Sorrow,
Endless story,
New tomorrow.

INDEX

C

D

E

F

G

H

I

J

K

L

M

N

S

W

X

Y

Z

ACKNOWLEDGMENTS

It is impossible to know where to start or end in acknowledging all those, living and dead, who played such an important part in the journey recounted in the following pages. I will, therefore, allow prudence and temperance to govern me and will desist from beginning the impossible task. I would, however, like to acknowledge my gratitude and indebtedness to the folks at Saint Benedict Press for putting their faith in my ability to bring this personal testimony to publishable fruition. I'd like to thank especially Robert and Conor Gallagher, Rick Rotondi, and Christian Tappe for their valued support and their practical labors in publishing this volume.

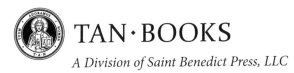